DR. TUVIA RINDE, PHD.

COMMON SENSE PRO

Proven principles for expert problem
solving and decision making

Producer & International Distributor
eBookPro Publishing
www.ebook-pro.com

Common Sense Pro
Dr. Tuvia Rinde, PhD.

Contact: Tuvia.Rinde@gmail.com
ISBN 9798683337476

COMMON SENSE PRO

Proven principles for expert problem
solving and decision making

DR. TUVIA RINDE, PHD.

CONTENTS

ACKNOWLEDGEMENTS AND THANKS

To you, dear people, events, places and instruments that appeared in my life—each with their own special surprises. To you, for each time of my falling into the illusion that everything was okay… something went wrong.

Thanks to my career and life as a consultant, I was capable of developing my observing and learning capabilities that apply to almost every place I find myself, all due to my simply being free from the immediate pressure of instant decisions.

To all those who explained things to me from their heightened levels of experience and professionalism; to those who determined things in the most decisive of manners, even when in cases they brought on the next set of errors or malfunctions; and so to you, theories from different disciplines, that though attempted to simplify and clarify matters, succeeded mostly in making them complicated and unresolved. I thank you.

Thus I walk around in this box of surprises called life, knowing that if everything goes off "without a hitch," it is nothing more than a miracle.

However, as the years pass, allowing for the time to look back at different events, it seems that there was the possibility to prevent most of "those problems".

And no! That is not a so simple and easy thing to understand.

I have been met with so many situations and events in which myth, beliefs, feelings, prejudice, habits, and experience all cause people to put away their practical wisdom and common sense... and so what if that can bring on a disaster?

Most of us are satisfied with returning to our routine when there is no explanation as to why the phenomenon appeared or disappeared. Sometimes the event... is not nice at all, and appears again at the least opportune time.

Many of us merely pray to be allowed to sail in the sea of life while promising to make any needed effort to bypass, or in the worst case, be able to live with the difficulties the obstacles present.

But then, what if we did get stuck without an outlet or solution? Perhaps then, in spite of it all, we'd be willing to employ some common sense or logic?

So, during a time I found myself stuck in an elevator, I decided, after more than a lot of years, to write the book of answers!

Thank you, dear elevator tech. You were the" final straw"! Thank you for not using your logic or common sense. don't fret, it always happens to well-experienced professionals.

If I can save more people from themselves or their surroundings with the help of my book "Common Sense for the

Advanced", allowing for their lives to be more predictable, filled with "positive boredom", safety, and joy, then, dear readers, I will be satisfied.

To those who enjoy uncertainty, troubles, and malfunctions merely for the fun of it and the spike of adrenalin it causes, please adopt the methodology that is handed over to you here so you can better plan the next exciting event.

I wish you a reading filled with smiles and pleasure at the offered exercises.

"Common Sense for the Advanced" will help you at work, outside activities, and even at home in the kitchen among the pots and pans. In short, it will affect all aspects of your life!

Dr. Tuvia Rinde, PhD.

THE END THAT BROUGHT ON
THE BEGINNING

They were two and a half days, during which I constantly asked myself "what next?" All the while, I pondered how it was forbidden to think "thoughts that invited problems and troubles."

It began minorly. As I was having my car treated in the garage, I asked the mechanic to check from where about a half-gallon of water kept disappearing every week, all without my seeing any leakage. He gave his answer in a very authoritative voice after a short observation, that according to his *experience*, the problem could only be caused by the charcoals from the water pump. It was a gradual process, he added, telling me he was sure it wouldn't stop me in the middle of the road.

So, how was it that I found myself the next morning able to travel only about one mile for every two gallons of water—water that was sprayed as hot jet from a hole in the rubber hose that in no time at all became a complete tear? I was ecstatic, since now the problem had matured and become a *big* problem—it was something they could diagnose! It would be easy to solve it.

The incredible thing was, that when I entered the garage and the hose was replaced, my dear mechanic said confidently that basing on his *ample experience*, the hole in the hose was not the cause for the loss of water. Instead, the main problem was the pump seals, and they will cause a surprise soon.

Clearly, as I was driving, my gaze hardly left the heat meter, leaving me constantly searching for steam from the engine compartment. Only very rarely would I actually look at the road and traffic.

The next problem occurred while I tried to drink a cup of coffee from my new kettle before sitting down to read my e-mails. In spite of following the whole preparation process, including having boiled the water numerous times exactly according to the manual, the taste of the coffee was disgusting. I can only assume that it was caused by the kettle cover having been made from sub-par materials.

I gave up on my need for coffee and instead came face to face with my computer that announced with red flashing letters that there were virus threats. There was also a written demand to press "clear". As a most obedient user, I found myself pressing again and again and again. At long last, after having completely given up, I called my technician, desperately asking for help. He took remote control of my computer, and so I was forced to spend the next two and a half hours keying different orders and staring at the screen. Eventually, the computer wouldn't even recognize the entrance passcode.

How wonderful! From a partial problem, it became a whole one. Only it turned out that my devoted technician had no idea what had happened—or even the reason for it. Exactly at the moment I was planning to call another expert, the problem was solved in an instant after he asked me to click on a few keys at the same time.

I found myself restless because yet again I had no idea what to expect from my computer, nor when the problem could appear again... and if it did appear, how to correct it.

Tired and dissatisfied, I drove to my grandchild's birthday. After having escaped from the celebrations with the feeling that I was a successful graduate of a "survival course " including magicians, turtles, candies and deafening noise, all I wanted was to drive calmly back home via the dark highway. Why then was it that suddenly a driver shouted out from his car beside me that I had a puncture. Where did that *come from*? I had just bought new all-terrain tires from a renowned manufacturer!

I replaced the huge tire with the help of my son, who I called because I was afraid to aggravate my back as I had hurt it the week before when I tried to fix the drain in the shower—but I won't exhaust you with that tale. Examining the tire at night did not expose the small tear I later found out about, and I remained optimistic about the possibility of repairing it completely.

The optimism faded when the guy at the tire repair shop the next morning gave me a pitiful look and said that if I had been smart enough not to drive more than half a mile on that tire, maybe there could have been a chance to save it. But now, the only option was to throw it away.

Again, a small problem had become a big one—and an expensive one, too.

It was a new morning and a beautiful sunny day. On my way to an important meeting in the city center, I felt optimistic about the chance of getting a new project. But, after only one mile, I found myself in a big traffic jam in a never-before blockaded country road!

Bypassing the traffic through dirt or back roads would not have been beneficial, and thus I was stuck at a constant pace of a maximum of ten miles an hour.

I hoped my luck would turn around once I got to my destination and I could simply park in the spot I knew they had reserved for me in the company parking lot. But with my eventual arrival, I saw that that was merely one more fantasy for reality to destroy.

There was a truck stuck right at the entrance to the company's lot, so once again I was driving aimlessly around the streets to look for parking.

After more than ten minutes and just shy of a minute from the scheduled meeting, I finally got a space. A drive that should have been no longer than an hour and a half, took almost three hours. The only reason I managed to reach the place semi-on time was because, as luck would have it, I had left early enough that morning.

After a short run to reach the elevator, and my pressing the button for the sixth floor, the doors closed then....

I found myself trapped in the elevator with a disabled command panel!

After a healthy and liberating laugh at my misfortune, I listened a few minutes to the people outside, hoping that somebody would notice that the elevator was stuck. Sadly, that was an entirely false hope.

A press on the alarm button created communication with the security man, though, to my surprise, he asked me in which elevator I was. How was that possibly something I could know? There was no number in the cage, and there were many elevators in the building.

Ten minutes passed from the time I was asked to relax and not to worry because, "We will take you out immediately," and I couldn't help but start to worry. I pressed again on the alarm button, and to my shock, the guy began to speak with me as if there had been no previous conversation.

"So, you are stuck?" he asked. "How long? Which elevator?"

He sounded like a good guy, and his intention was definitely to help... but my experience dictated that I had to decrease my expectations. The rescue would take time.

I pulled out the flash-light that is always in my bag, ready if the lights go off. I had noticed that the ventilator wasn't working; it was starting to get hot and I knew it would only get hotter. I tried to check the ceiling and to open the door, but without success. I finally noticed a small cover with a label with the word telephone on it. Joy! There was a phone inside! When I picked up the earpiece with a hope to reach somebody who held a bit of common sense, I found myself speaking with the same guy.

He was once more really nice and full of empathy, and

when he asked me *again*, being as it had been forty minutes since out previous conversation: "Are you really trapped in the elevator?"—(Kafka, if he could have come back to life, would have surely died at that)— "It will take a few minutes to get it open and get you out. Be patient," he told me.

Few minutes later he asked me if I was in elevator number eight or nine. It took insurmountable self-control to tell him that, to the best of my memory, I was in the first elevator from the right side.

He suddenly shouted, "How come? Impossible! The elevator is going through maintenance." I answered that I simply walked in through the door. I heard him mumbling to himself that the control board showed that all the elevators were okay, all except the one in maintenance, and I probably went into number nine, *but number 9 was in order!*

Now I was very close to the conclusion that *I* did not exist!

I asked him to call the manager I had the meeting with and to let her know that I was late. I also told him—very firmly—to call a technician and to instruct him to check *all* the elevators.

At long last, I heard the fireman opening the emergency lock and opening the door. The security man was speaking to himself loudly, saying that he couldn't understand why elevator number eight was flashing in the control board as number nine; that he couldn't understand why no one had put up a sign that the elevator was under maintenance; and that he didn't understand how the technician on the roof connected the electricity *for one moment,* long enough to allow me to get into the elevator. He was also clearly surprised to see a man come out of an elevator after having been locked in for gods knew how long, laughing and amused.

He received an answer only for the last question.

I was laughing because I felt thankful to *you*, dear security man, because you pushed me to sit down and write as soon as possible the book that had been building in my mind, waiting for me to write it, all my life.

"COMMON SENSE FOR THE ADVANCED"

Though you may have the impression this is the end of the story, I assure you, it is not.

When I entered the manager's office—more than an hour passed the planned time—I was told that the manager I had expected to meet was sick and that she had instructed another colleague to meet me. however, she was not in the office because she had been informed that I was in the elevator and had gone down to the entrance to meet me. She had left without her cellphone, so the worker in the adjacent office could not inform her that I had arrived.

Using my common sense, I decided to wait. After about fifteen minutes, she came in and was surprised to meet me. I started laughing again and introduced myself as the elevator survivor. That was when she claimed that I could simply not be who I said I was, because according to her best and most recently updated information, *I was still in the elevator*!

My hope is that after smiling and feeling a little pity because of this anecdote, you also accepted and understood the importance of using our common sense—and of using it frequently: Sometimes, in order to prevent future risks or problems, sometimes so we can fulfill our goals, and, in most cases, to maneuver yourself out from events, problems and\or risks with less harm.

I wish to provide you with the logic and capability to manage, predict, and avoid risks, and so too to reduce harmful fallouts from mistakes and events.

While reading, we shall encounter all the stages in the life-cycle process of malfunctions or risks. We shall learn to use our logic correctly and methodically in every step, to later process that in order for it to help us manage our intentions, plans, risks and surprises with the leadership brought on by systematic and logical use of common sense.

The image depicted below, presents the eleven-step process that we shall undergo. We will be able to take full advantage of it when we will be capable of using each ability immediately, in every given situation.

The speed of our thought, especially when we are trained and act semi-automatically, is much faster than the speed of any movement or speech, thus we can use the common sense methodology for stressful situations and for long-durational planning.

THE LEADING STEPS FOR CONDUCTING YOURSELF WITH COMMON SENSE

The methodology we will scan together while moving from step to step in the direction of the arrow.

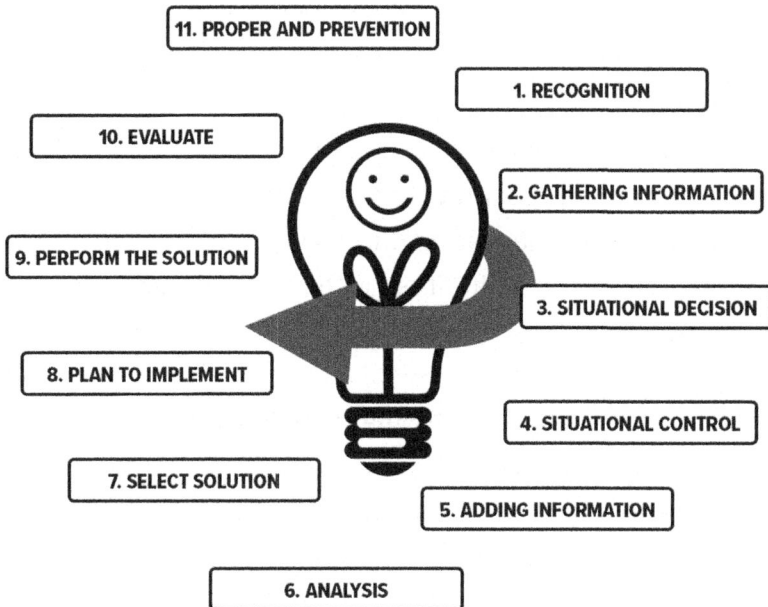

I am aware of the fact that there are unclear stages. During your study of this book, you shall adopt the ability to activate common sense methodology on a daily basis.

Later, after absorbing the basic logical tools, we will be able to improve our abilities further by managing every stage while using more supporting tools.

We shall begin with learning how to activate our improved common sense while managing faults and events. Future chapters will relate to the need of prediction.

In every fault or event there are two components:

1. A factor, or few factors, which happened in the past and are currently influencing the present. Factors where we try to avoid harmful outcomes and to ensure continuing benefits in the future.
2. Factors that present a deviation from what is perceived as normal and ordered. In so meaning, we hold a clear picture of the target, of the needed corrections, and of returning the situation to the normal and wanted standard.

For example: the tooth ache that radiates from the hole you "worked hard" to create for years through eating sweets, is now in need of an urgent filling and root canal treatment. If delayed, I could potentially lose the tooth completely.

Or: A great joy that brought on a loss of control, that subsequently made you say to your mother in law\aunt\ wife's brother your *real* opinion—the same opinion that you'd avoided expressing for years while remaining in tight control and staying "politically correct."

More complexity is added when there is a need of prediction since:

- There is a need to plan and create new substance, a new entity, or a future reality.
- There is a need for tools to set the wanted target so that the future will be defined as the normal mode.
- It causes us to act in an environment of uncertainty because there is no preconceived, comparable notion as to what the correct situation is.
- There are risks on the way, and there is also the requirement to avoid unwanted changes that will build additional stumbling blocks.

For example: Your father told you happily when you were about eight years old that he was *surprise...* when you reached that age, you found that there was enough money only to buy a front door.

Or: While reading one of the books that promise a "recipe for success", you are stuck, humiliated with yourself, because you aren't able to immediately answer the question of what you would like to do in five years. Hello, guys! *I* don't know what will be or what I want for *tomorrow*!

Bellow you will find more almost "routine" examples from our everyday life, starting with technical, family, and even romantic problems. **We shall use them for demonstrating** failures in our way of thinking, and for exercising the advanced common sense cognitive logic.

The chance to think straight and effectively will develop in time.

THE OBSTACLES IN THE WAY TOWARD "ADVANCED COMMON SENSE."

Common sense is commonly defined in the dictionaries as the "mental ability to think, consider, and evaluate for the purpose of achieving something." It differs greatly from feelings and emotions.

A **"healthy brain"** is commonly defined as capable of simple, rational thinking, and of reaching a reasonable conclusion.

Reasonable means having the ability to understand and explain things logically and in a convincing way, while basing the analysis on the science of logic, honest thinking, and the right organization of things.

The test is always the ability to explain the syllogism, connection and influence between different things. Said ability brings correct and progressive understanding. It means that we have reached a higher level of comprehension than we possessed at the starting step.

We shall proceed slowly in our search for advanced common sense, and we shall clear the mines that are embedded in us and are, too, a natural part of the toolbox we live with. It is a toolbox that is used to interpret reality or what *we perceive* as a reality.

A most amusing or, alternately, sad situation occurs when we look at ourselves while meeting a surprise that is unfamiliar and far from controlled. In these times, we are very far from our best, and we run through all sorts of reactions and actions until we eventually accept what is really needed to be effective.

I have met, quite frequently, with the partial or even total absence of logical common sense, even in planned, initiated and controlled activities.

A few examples that many of us meet in our lives:

The faults and problem producer:
I am accustomed to finding the diesel fuel pump in the left side of the pump's position. Why then did someone all of a sudden switch the sides? I found myself filling up my car with petrol instead of diesel. Never mind the money, I was afraid that the engine would blow! Did I act with my common sense? No! I found myself acting by the force of an *automatic habit.*

The faults and problems increaser:
How many of us press the household fuse over and over when our electric kettle stops boiling the water, and eventually sit in darkness for a few hours, waiting until the power company technician arrives to save us from ourselves and

correct the main fuse at the entrance to the house? Did we use common sense? *No*! We were simply eager to drink a hot cup of tea on a cold night.

The failure transferrer:
When we called the plumber to correct the wetness on the wall, he said that he had to replace a section of the pipe that was rusted and cracked. So, why only about half a year later, wetness appeared also under the floor? Oh, Yes! The plumber took care of his future income. The new section was wider and with greater wall thickness. Because of that, the water pressure in another old and rusted section became narrower, thus increasing its diameter, and causing another crack and flooding. **Are we aware of the fact that in many cases, correcting failures creates or accelerates additional failures?**

Was common sense activated? Yes, when regarding the point of interest of the plumber, but not when we consider the interest of the client—or even the pipe! All in all, the problem was transferred from one place and time to another and in so ensuring the client paid twice with no reason.

By the way, we have similar problems in the financial angles. It happens every time the banker offers us a loan to settle debts, with both of us knowing full well my continual ability to pay the installments—"the radiant of the pipe" would eventually leave me with bigger debt and even less of an ability to cover it.

Faults replicator:

The computer technician who checked my silent computer, was sure that the broken part was the sound card. He plugged in a new one but nothing happed, so he plugged in another. Three damaged cards were needed until he realized that the voltage connected to the bay was not in order. He was right about diagnosing the symptoms, but he missed identifying the cause, thus losing all the potential profit from this visit.

Did he activate logical common sense? No! He used an ancient method, the method of trying and being wrong again and again—carrying on the pattern until succeeding. A method based on his best experience.

Is it us or professionals who we trust, those who have learned mechanics or electricity or medicine or economics, so mindless? Either we don't use common sense in the right time, or we continually look for shortcuts.

Let us invite ourselves on a tour in the toolbox we have collected during years of development, and see what most of our tools are:

Knowledge: General education that we have gathered from reading, experience, and the people we interact with. Part of the knowledge is imparted through orderly education, and other parts are compiled as pieces of information from different disciplines.

For example: we can assume that most of us know that gold doesn't get rusty, even if we are not chemists; or that fat hurts the heart despite us not being doctors; and alternatively, there is a high probability that a father who beats his children or wife, was himself battered as a child—knowledge you have even if you are not a social worker.

Professionalism: Most of us will define this as specializing and focusing on specific content.

For example: the orthopedist is an expert concerning musculoskeletal structures, and nothing bur; or the banker who exclusively works with foreign exchange trading; or the computer technician who knows how to fix HP computers alone.

Experience: Most commonly defined as the sum of the memories and lessons from the events we have experienced. Being a theater actor who has acted for thirty years as a silent tree, means that we can assume he is an old timer. But it will also be hard to believe that the actor is capable of a variety of other roles—roles that include either dramatic or comic undertones, or that singing, or dancing capabilities are expected. On the other hand, I am sure you will agree that if somebody has worked only two years in a small CPAs office where he did bookkeeping, balance sheets, auditing, and even had discussed and negotiated with the assenting officer for his clients, then we can assume he holds a great variety of experiences that enable him to establish an independent business for himself. **He has real and valuable experience.**

Skill: The ability to transfer theoretical knowledge to practical uses in the best way possible.

If you were staring jealously at the hands of a cook who was cutting vegetables with movements so fast you could barely see his hands moving, or if you were listening enviously to a singer giving a fantastic performance without breaking a sweat, or perhaps watching a painter painting the wall smoothly without allowing even one drop to fall to the floor, it means that you were watching the results of skilled experts who had exercised the same activities thousands of times. They eventually improved to perfection the coordination and planning between their brains and hands—or other parts—and the materials and tools needed to execute their crafts.

Relationship, acquaintance and the networking support that you maintain with family, friends, and colleagues, offer you the ability to share your problems and dilemmas and to get some good advice or practical help. It will happen only if you will be ready to **put aside your ego** without letting it stop you because of feelings such as "I will respect myself only if I will solve the problem alone," "My wife will appreciate me much more if…" or, alternatively, I will prove to myself again than I am better than others

Intuition: The mysterious process that occurs in our head and leads us to estimate, assume, or decide about causes and solutions for the problem that we try to handle. We are not able to teach or imitate it, because we don't know how it works. We can, however, indicate that in most of the times that we encountered high-levels of intuition, it was based on a high level of professionalism combined with a lot of diverse experience. We see that the typical situation presented is that the intuition is tuned to one field and not spread out to multidisciplinary areas. For one person it is a developed ability to feel and asses reliability and integrity of people, for the other, it is the ability to directly access the real causes of a fault in an engine while not relying solely on the exposed, visible symptoms.

People say that if you have a great intuition, you don't need to use common sense and logic. Sorry, only a very few of us have a high level of intuition, and even for them, it does not apply a good answer for every part of life.

Advanced common sense is the ability to understand and explain things in a logical and convincing manner, one based on the science of logic, integrity, honest thinking, and the right organizing of concepts that helps explain the mutual connections and influence between phenomenon.

Common sense is apparently one more tool in the toolkit.

Actually, it is also the total toolbox in which we put in all the other abilities.

It is also the process supplier that enables a systematic and consistent way for problem solving and making decisions based on past faults and for future predictions—provided it is used in the right way.

If, for instance, our friend the security man who left me trapped din the elevator for so long had used a little more common sense—and used it correctly—all while still not touching on *advanced* common sense, he would have been able to reach the solution as to how to release me after merely the first ring of the alarm bell.

> **We are equipped with wonderful tools...** *so what*?
>
> **Many of the times, the tools we have developed to build success are the tools that can cause our failures.**

For example: Over the time in which we have accumulated collective experiences from our parents and grandparents, we have also adopted "interesting habits." One such example is the lady who executed an emergency stop with her car because she saw a black cat crossing the road. Maybe she would have had a huge success in avoiding the bad luck that incident alone could have brought on but, at the same time, she heard the hard hit of the car from behind her ramming into her car because he had had no time to stop! She based her actions on her collective experience... *so what*?

Another example could be the knowledgeable doctor who updates himself regarding all the forecasts of viruses and diseases in his region, then when Mr. George came in sneezing and coughing, the doctor looked at him with a pleasant and self-confident smile and, to be sure, asked if George had low fever. After hearing the positive answer he expected, he sent him back home to rest with the determination that he had flu—the same as everybody in the town. *Doctor, one moment, please!* George didn't tell you—and you didn't ask—that during that afternoon he had sprayed against pests and insects, a poison spray, with a very pungent smell. **Basically, the doctor was leaning on**

irrelevant information!

And, the guy who fears cellphone antenna radiation and fights to reduce the output power of the transmitters to "decrease the environmental risk!" Our innocent friend did not know, or did not relate to the fact that when there is a weak signal strength, the cellphone in his hand interprets the matter as him being far away from the radio relay. Thus, it increases its own transmitting power, resulting in the guy's brain "roasting and cooking" from his own phone. The guy was using professional but partial knowledge and made a huge mistake because **he did not identify the interactions between the system components.**

Or, the unclear intuition that causes me to have doubts about doing business with men who are short, fat, bald, and with mustaches. Perhaps the reason is because they are so similar to the sergeant major who gave me a hell during the basic training in the army, but the bottom line is, **I used my intuition and I likely made a big mistake!**

A final example could be the financial advisor who was happy to support my investing decisions again and again. Did he do it because it was good for me? Or maybe because it was better for him?

> **The inevitable conclusion from all the examples is that:**
> **Every ability can also be a limitation unless it is led**
> **through advanced common sense.**

> ## THE TARGET!
>
> **Common sense for the advanced will provide tools for:**
>
> - Better recognition of risks or faults in every aspect of life.
> - Increasing the likelihood and confidence in getting benefits from our plans.
> - Avoiding or reducing possible damages when faults or events happen.
> - Minimum recovery time so investments can function again.
> - Prevention of repeating of the same mistakes regarding identifying, diagnosing or solving problems.
> - Avoiding complications, solving problems, and preventing additional ones.

In order to derive the maximum benefit, it is strongly recommended to put your ego aside, to let it rest, and to tell it not to interfere. It is very useful to put the ego on the shelf every time you intend to check yourself and test your ability to manage and handle events, plans, surprises and crises that happen in your life.

So too, it is recommended to read a chapter or even less at a time, and to try to learn from the examples and exercises. Please try to choose different kinds of events from your daily life, then try the challenge of using the advanced common sense method to analyze and solve them.

I am sure that you will find you are improving your ability step by step.

Try to do this by using humor and a smile. I promise that in addition to enabling your toolbox to be equipped with handling advanced common sense, you will add joy into your daily life, and improve your quality of living. It is worthwhile to share the lessons with others as well, since more ways of thinking bring on more options for problem solving. There is one condition to fulfill, and that is keeping an open mind and being ready to listen with mutual respect.

Those who want to look perfect or those who are shy, be aware of the possibility of learning alone. Just be ready to be open and honest with yourself, and show readiness not to be fixed and tied to your habits, beliefs, and preconceived stereotypes

WHAT DOES A PROBLEM OR MALFUNCTION MEAN FOR US?

Let us move on and ask: What is a problem or a fault—or an event or risk factor? How do we define to ourselves that we have a problem, or that we are in the middle of the process of solving it?

It seemed to me, that the taxi driver was very angry as he drove across the badly paved road from my office to my home. To my question as to what had happened, he answered with a mumble, that "this car is an old buggy." The day before, the car had functioned with additional power, all while taking less gas.

Let us agree that the driver knows and remembers how the car was yesterday and the day before that. The driver was able to recognize that it was running differently, that something was wrong. **That the car was running in a lower form from the standard that the driver was accustomed to.**

If we generalize the definition of deviating from the "normal and proper situation" and face the fact that from the minute that something happens to us—something that stimulates our feelings, interests, or worries, causes us to feel confusion, or even leaves us in dangerous or challenging scenarios—we are in a state of possible, and sometimes inevitable failure. This is a change that brings the risk that we will not be able to come back or maintain the situation that is interpreted as normal, or alternatively, the standard.

It is important to remember that the standard is the situation that is the base for conducting the ongoing daily life, even if it is not necessarily the ultimate, desirable goal. For example, I am satisfied with living in a rented apartment, as long as the renter is sane. The rent is fair, and all the furniture and instruments are in order. However, in the future, I hope to own an apartment, myself. My belief is that you can easily find those who live a satisfactory and peaceful life, at ease with their current reality, and then there are the others—those who constantly feel mounting frustration and simmering failure at the fact that they don't have an apartment of their own.

I assume that you will agree with the notion that as long as only emotional therapy is in power, nothing will be solved! Emotional therapy is often the accelerator for change, but we have to call for the advanced common sense to lead us in a systematic and consistent way in order for us to achieve an effective solution.

I will note—with a philosophical smile—that there are exceptions, specifically in situations where we are lacking in motivation or lack of sense of self-ability to bring about any form of change, be it because the fault is a great solution to another problem that has not yet been solved, or perhaps because it is simply too stressful, or because it is much more beneficial to stay with the current situation.

For example: John is very worried about failing an exam, and ends up getting a high fever that will not pass until well after the exam date. Or, a malfunction in the door lock that makes it impossible to lock the house—a malfunction that "saved" me from going to an opera I did not want to go to in the first place. In a lot of case people are not aware of their subconscious influence on their behavior.

> **A fault means a deviation from the standard.**
>
> **Deviation from a defined and agreed upon action.**
>
> **We will never be able to detect deviations in our design and reality without our knowing the correct functioning thar is required**

> **You should also remember that the willingness to act in order to change reality is based on the Rejection and dissatisfaction with the existing situation.**
> **On one side, and Attraction and a desire to achieve a proper state of a perceivable, possible achievement on the other.**

In other words. Not every deviation from standard will trigger action. Sometimes, the change in reality is perceived as desirable—even though it has deviated from the norm. It is then that we make every effort to continue to live with the "positive problem." This is a perfect example as to why you would need common sense.

Let's get into the thick of it, while assuming we usually choose *not* to continue living with problems and faults—at least not those we perceive as ones we are capable and are interested in solving!

The group of mishaps and risks is a "clan" of many participants, all with a variety of families. Some are objective and some are only in our minds and thoughts. If we do not deal with them correctly, we will not be able to find a solution. Some of them are malfunctions and risks that we must continue to live with.

Let's get to know the main types:

A malfunction from another time: The fact that you discovered the fault *now*, does not mean that it was born now!

For example: The car was returned to the parent company to repair a malfunction that was brought about during the production process.

A malfunction from another place: The fact that you discovered the problem *here* does not mean that it was born here!

For example: a pollution carried through streams and rivers, "born" in a forest dozens of kilometers away, reached the ocean and caused great harm.

A "life partner" fault. Ongoing and unsolved: The fact that you discovered the problem does not mean that you can correct it. Perhaps the best decision would be to continue living with it.

For example: The fact that you are constantly on the defense when it comes to your mother-in-law.

For example: Your car is recorded on a speedometer that it can reach a speed of 150 miles per hour, but every time you try, you find that your car cannot go over 80.

The "symptomatic" problem, which *looks* like a problem, but is actually the side-effect that you cannot or do not want to start "digging" through in order to try and find the cause.

For example: When steam comes out of your car engine, the steam can perhaps be a symptom of a lack of water or a leakage. Or, perhaps due to you wanting to save and not buying a coolant? Or even because of your poor discipline when it comes to the question of checking the water levels in the cooling tank?

The" failing problem" is a problem that, as time passes, decreases in intensity and influence, and sometimes disappears as if never being.

For example: a water leakage from the kitchen faucet—specifically from the hose's connection—diminishing over time. The plumber, who you had previous experience, knew that, so it only needed sealing tape additional time to acclimatize and eventually stop the drip.

The growing problem. As time goes by, power accumulates, and symptoms and damage intensify.

For example: the increase use of headache reliever, though reduces symptoms, also forces you to up the required dosage over time and lean more heavily on drugs.

Malfunction—in the eyes of the beholder: It appears that in many of the situations we encounter, the concept of "malfunction" is not completely agreed upon. Two people examining the same phenomenon may result in a situation in which one believes whole heartedly that everything is in order, while the other sees nothing but deviations and risks.

For example: I ordered a cup of coffee in a restaurant. It was served with great grace, but it was cold! All attempts to make it warmer failed because the coffee temperature standard of the Italian planner of the machine was very low compared with the drinking habits here. To him it was right, but in my eyes, it was a severe malfunction.

Now comes the time to ask in-depth questions regarding how each of us work.

When and how does one think they should exercise advanced common sense?

Automation against the activation of common sense:

In the middle of the morning, I asked myself what was order I used to get dressed? Would I first put on my socks? Or perhaps I usually put on my pants or shirt? Later, I realized that I could not remember the number of intersections I passed on my way to work, nor if the lights were red or green. I also vaguely remembered that at the entrance to the kitchenette in the offices, I met many people who wished me a good morning—though perhaps they also said something else... *but I couldn't remember*!

It seemed that I did not leave the state of automation until at least an hour and a half after arriving at work; and even then, it was only after realizing that the paperwork I had left on my desk the day before and was expecting to find where I had left it, was in fact, not there.

I assume that the phenomenon is familiar to us all. We've all had a variation of it at some point—be it by putting the house or car keys in a place we never remember, or wondering if we locked the house door.

I accept and understand that there is no chance that we would remain sane and focused on more important things if for every action we would direct a lot of attention and brain power—so too for every process accompaniment, method analyzation, and being able to reach eventual correct solutions. Hopefully, we are aware of the fact that we are sleeping, or rather, working automatically, and therefore we soon possess a mechanism, a kind of sleep breaker that moves us to awakening and thinking intelligently a moment before—and not a moment after—the appearance of reason / risk / action. Factors that require us to use an intelligent activity that we should know how and when to activate.

Anyone who traveled many miles before discovering they were driving with a boiling engine because of the absence of water, only because the routine of "sleeping during driving," did not include a recurring scan of the heat clock. I'm sure they remember and understand what it is about, if only because of the unpleasant experience of getting towed from a main road that was accompanied by a "big fine" in the form of payment to the garage.

Anyone who found out that they'd missed the intersection where they'd planned to get off the highway only after a few miles and only after finishing the romantic phone call they'd previously been busy with, would recognize that the distraction from driving and the road itself was at the level of automatic driving.

The moment when we ask ourselves, I'm so alert and intelligent, and what now? Will be the moment when we embark on an effective use of **" advanced common sense.""**.

First, we will examine ourselves and see what is the breaker that stimulates us. Understanding its activity is important to us for future and present benefits.

Take for example a familiar example to us all: while driving at a constant speed on a two-way road, a vehicle bypasses us despite the proximity of vehicles in the opposite lane, and in another second he tries to fit back on the track, right in front of us! What goes on in our heads during those seconds

? Did we identify the situation and were we alert enough to the risk? Or were we looking for a station on the radio or a phone number?

Assuming we identified the situation, did the vision of the circumvention create an immediate and intentional change to anything in our driving style? And if so, in which direction? Should we continue to travel and run "justice" (which comes from emotion) and let the person who overtook pay the price for his behavior? Or, perhaps we should slow down and let them fit in safely? And, after you decided to slow down, did you invest the planning and thinking about how to do it intelligently, all without being a part of risk?

If we freeze in those seconds, we will see that in order to get out of the situation safely (without the help of luck, something that is always helpful), we need to correctly and wisely process a number of stages of diagnosis, decisions, and executions!

Consider the familiar moment of entering the subway car, where in a second you have found yourself as a single normative creature in a car with a half-drunk, noisy bunch. What would go through your head in those seconds? Did you identify the situation and were you aware of the risk?

After the first identification, we need to follow a step-by-step process for several stages of diagnosis, resolution, resolution, and execution!

In these dangerous cases, we do not have the "right" to

use the **"trial and error"** approach, which usually leads to increased troubles.

Those who work in the "try and make a mistake" approach, or as some call it, a "successful method" (sometimes successful and sometimes not), based on the existence of a huge bank of time, money, materials, spare parts and more, are invited to stop reading here! But, most of us do not have this luxury, not in regard to our professional lives, and not in personal one.

The steps that are right and proper for us to go through within seconds and sometimes fractions of seconds are:

1. **Being alert and being able to give meaning to existing information. Or alternatively, continue gathering information and search for meaning.**
2. **Making a decision mode! Usually regarding prevention or reduction of damage and or increasing benefits.**
3. **Mapping all components of the events while trying to understand the whole picture and identifying the effects and interrelations among the components.**
4. **Analysis and detection of factors. (Not the symptoms / side effects))4.**
5. **Finding possible solutions in view of the identified factors.**
6. **Selection and implementation of the applicable solution, depending on the existence and availability of means.**

7. **Preventing or reducing the chance of repeated error or risk.**

We can pass through all the stages in less than a second because the speed of our thoughts is hundreds of times faster than the speed in which we talk or act. It depends if you treat yourself as capable of managing the situation without frizzing and feeling only numbness. It seems to be easy... Not yet!

We have to learn how to do every step in the proper way. Skipping stages will cause us to deviate from the road of the advanced common sense. But, before we learn how to use and do every step and process of the advanced common sense, we must have a meeting with ourselves for the sake of understanding how we are built and what in us will allow or prevent the ability to act in a very focused and consistent way together with common sense.

How do we interpret reality and act?

What is going through your mind when you hear that sentence?

I cannot stand it anymore, I will surely faint! All that red *is poured all over the floor and the dog is stretched out without moving. Please help, save him, do something!*

In that scenario, one will call ambulances immediately, one for animals and the second for people.

The other will look desperately at the floor that was just

washed only two hours ago, and will be very angry at the dog that poured the raspberry juice everywhere.

The third will be amused and surprised at how the dog could sleep so peacefully in every place—even in this wet mess.

I imagine that you have also encountered in your life examples and illustrations of the fact that it is not only the sight and the voices that determine interpretation to a particular reality. **People tend to interpret the same data differently as a result of the influence of different interests or cultural backgrounds.** We will have to take into account that in any activity involving reciprocal relations with people, it is necessary to examine how people interpret our activities, and vice versa.

I will be happy if you will agree to adopt the insight that follows from this next conclusion:

> **Fantasy is what I think and how I value myself.**
>
> **Reality is what others think and how they value me.**
>
> **The inevitable conclusion is that**
>
> **My reality = the fantasy of the others!**
>
> **There is no "absolute truth" in a mutual relationship**
>
> **But we will never give up any effort to learn and know**
>
> **How we are perceived by our surroundings.**

Think about your last meeting with your insurance agent

who sold you much more insurance that you need because he succeeded to identify your fears along with the absorption of the trust and esteem you feel towards him. **His reality is your fantasy!**

Or, come with me to the industry to meet an electrician, who is known as the main factory troubleshooter, and thus surprised me when, as a reaction to a simple call that came in at 14:50, he said to the director of the facility "look, it is very complicated and will take a long time to correct, it is preferred to do it in the morning when we have a whole day before us."

How? How does the facility director not notice that he was already on his way home? He simply did not want to stay and work.

> **When using a human resource to collect information, analyze or solve, it is very useful to be aware of the interests and attitudes of the source.**
>
> **The toolmaker or electrician are not a voltmeter or vibration meter or a thermometer that is indifferent to the information it provides and the effects it may have.**

If you ever tried to get a recipe from your mother in law for the cake that her dear son (your husband) loves, you have encountered the same phenomenon. In some cases, you even received a card with "exact" baking instructions.

So, why then that when you followed the instructions it did not work at all? You are in trouble!

If you noticed the little hidden smile or the tiny spark of gloating in your mother-in-law's eye, you would understand that you were led into a trap that creates a wonderful opportunity for her to show her superiority over her "less talented" daughter-in-law, all despite her having "made every effort" to guide you...

There are secrets in life you never discover! Not from your mother-in-law and not from the toolmaker!

These amusing or annoying examples bring us to the first chapter that we should learn how to follow in the path of the advanced common sense. The chapter of

Awareness and alertness on giving meaning to existing or to-be-collected information.

THE INITIAL INFORMATION

When I got stuck with my car in the middle of the road and the only thing that worked consistently was the flashing lights on the dashboard, I realized that there was no way I could handle, overcome and solve the problem, I decided to order a tow truck to take me to the garage. I was even satisfied that I made and had a tow insurance policy.

Now, there is a question as to where the phone number is written? The answer was easy because I remembered that I wrote it on a note that I put in my wallet. Or maybe it was written on the insurance certificate in the glove compartment, where I always leave the certificate of the previous year. Just to be sure.

What next? Self-surprise!

I left the license wallet at home, and I only had with me the wallet with money.

(Really... What I needed then was a little more pressure—being stuck without the driving license. Perhaps I would even get the additional joy of a ticket). I took the old insurance certificate out of the glove compartment and dialed the tow center.

Seven attempts to get through to them in twenty minutes later, and then finally getting through to talk with a polite service representative, I was told that a year ago I was insured, but that this year, I was not.

She thought that maybe this year my insurance agent bought me the dragging insurance from another company. Now I had to get ahold of my insurance agent at 22:00 PM. I had no choice, so I dialed and luckily, I caught him in the middle of a wedding party. The devoted man told me that he did not remember where I was insured, but he did remember that there was a change because he searched for a cheaper deal.

The next step was that I waited for one hour until my dear agent would pass through his office on his way home and give me the details. Afterwards, it took the tow track two more hours to come. At about 02:00 AM, we reached the closed gate of the garage and I decided

To stay and sleep in the car. It was not appropriate or polite to ask my friend, the garage owner, to get out of bed at 01:30 to open the gate for me, something which was definitely reasonable at 22:30.

Why did this happen to me?

Because I have committed a huge "crime," consisting of three sins! And this is in addition to the original sin of having the idea that **"it will not happen to me"** that is characteristic to many of us.

The giant "crime" is that I did not maintain the information and did not prepare myself for the possibility that I would need it. It includes three sins:

The information is out of date, not reliable, and not easily available.

No, please do not swallow a pitying smile. Instead, ask yourself if you have an available and up-to-date information about the ownership of your house, health security, warranty of your electrical instruments and more. And, you probably don't remember when your passport expires.

I'm hopeful that you left me here and went to check at least one of the subjects that were mentioned or similar ones. After you have dealt with everything, you most likely think that we can continue. **But the answer is no!** First of all, you must do two necessary actions that will prevent the repetition of the three sins—at least in all current issues that you may encounter during your daily life.

> **1. Create an updated database.**
>
> **2. Set an updating data feed routine.**

I am aware that the first setup can take a lot of time, especially when doing it thoroughly, but you will very soon find out how much time and pressure it will save you in times of trouble.

For example, organizing relevant information that supports your activities in the most basic way (which will be refined later) according to four categories, such as: Home; Work; Traffic; going out with friends.

Friends	Work	Traffic	Home
List of clubs	Code list	Towing phone	Concierge phone
Entertain-ment sites	Pizzeria phone	Insurance phone	Maintenance phone
Regular activities	Phone of computer support	Train schedule	TV operating guide
Member card binder	Birthday of the boss	Car book	Plumbing plan
Wallet of discount coupons	Parking lot phone	Speed radar	Dishwasher guide

Of course, you are invited to customize and build your data according to your preferences. You should also remember to store them in the appropriate place for its needs and uses. The phone number for the towing company should be in the car and not merely a magnet on the door of the refrigerator. The vouchers purse should preferably be in the shopping bag, not on the desk at work.

And yes, please remember that when you enter the elevator, you should have a flashlight and you should watch and check its number and the location of the emergency phone and button.

Exercise 1: please take a pen and a piece of paper and write down all the information and equipment that you will need available to you before and during your next trip that you intend to make.

Things get complicated when we learn that these seemingly apparent facts have different meanings and interpretations from different pairs of "glasses" that people wear when they look at reality.

For one woman, mink fur is a symbol of prestige, though for the other, it is a symbol of inhumanity. For one man, smoking a smoking pipe is a status symbol, and for the other, it means lack of consideration and sensitivity. I remember for years the insurance agent's guide who explained to his students in the sales course that they had to "break up and defrost the relationship" before getting to business. "Compliment the picture, the furniture or something else." In the next meeting, one of the students stood up and spoke about the compliment he had given to a potential client about the beautiful picture hanging on the wall near his desk. The customer responded angrily and said it was his mother-in-law's gift from when he opened the office and that he hates her and her picture, but, he does not want to get into trouble with her because she visits the office a lot. The agent was perceived as having the same taste as the mother-in-law. There was no chance of a sale there!

The examples illustrate the need to develop the ability to distinguish between different types of information that belong to different perceptions of so-called reality, be it of ourselves or others. The distinction will help to focus and exercise **common sense,** primarily in recognizing our own and others' attitudes to facts and information, something which seems to be identical. We will do this by acquiring the ability to identify and use **the three types of lenses** through which we look at reality.

THE THREE GLASSES APPROACH

One day, when my good friend Norman—who was married—and I met, I asked with a smile if he wanted to have a lover. He turned pale and silent. Since then, he made every effort not to be alone with me, not even for one minute. I really did not understand what I had done until Scott, our mutual friend, wanted to meet me to ask for advice on how to help Norman bring to an end the relationship with his lover. Scott added that Norman was already "tired" of her, but she frightened him, and he was afraid to be blackmailed. *Surprise*!

It took me a few seconds to realize what a pit I had fallen into with my innocent question to Norman back then. Thanks, my friends, you have given me a nice gift. Now, I have the chance to explain to you, my readers, and to myself, how to avoid similar mishaps when simply wanting to collect information.

When a person acts and relates to the world, he can do so through **three different pairs of "glasses."** Those who stand in front of him are not always clear on which pair he acts upon and when he wears each. This issue itself is a source of mishaps or misunderstandings, even before we start dealing with the real problems and failures.

So, let's do preventive monitoring to get rid of unnecessary problems that prevent us from getting to the information and data we need.

First pair of eyeglasses: the "need" glasses!

When your mother looked at you with penetrating eyes when you came to a holiday dinner with your children, *her* (!) grandchildren, and in a sing-song voice said, "You have to behave politely and chew with your mouth closed." What do you understand from that?

When the priest or the rabbi read the commandment "Do not commit adultery," and each remembers where they left their umbrellas they were looking for— What did *they* understand?

When the plant engineer told the operator that the pump was planned to transfer while at full capacity 2500 cubic meters of fuel per hour, and the operator laughed and said he never dares to transfer more than 1,200 cubic meters so it would not fall to pieces, what do you understand?

> **When someone acts and speaks from the "necessary" position, he wants to reflect standards—a metric criteria—according to which he measures your behavior and activity, or wants to determine for you how to behave.**

In most cases, "necessary" activity stems from religion,

beliefs, ideology, ethos, or a particular culture—be it social, managerial, or professional. You will encounter this when your company manager trains you to function to achieve maximum quality and customer satisfaction. You will see it when you will be forced to separate different kinds of trash for the sake of recycling in the name of ideas about the need of the preservation of the Earth.

The efforts to influence that are operated through **the "need" approach** and can be agreed and accepted or denied and rebelled against. But, first and foremost, it is imperative to identify them! Especially since in many cases they are cleverly disguised with great sophistication.

Second pair of eyeglasses: "Want."
"I feel I like it," is the common phrase that appears dozens of times during the day among children who still have the freedom of expression and lack of control. I feel, I like, and I want it, reflects the pure desire to have an ice cream, ride a motorcycle, jump on a trampoline, or tour around the world. This is the cleanest expression of **"desire and willing"** that reflects the interest. But—and there is always a but somewhere—the longer the interest becomes, the more the way to achieve it involves and includes efforts that meet other's interests, ones that are occasionally in opposition to it. The interest owner learns that sometimes, hiding their wants is more beneficial.

Again, it is important to understand that identifying the "pair of glasses," the original position through which the other side of ourselves looks and his attitude

or interest at the situation, is always helpful.

For example, when a peer manager tells you that he has to increase the team by five people, otherwise he will not withstand the workload, and you suspect that the motivation comes from a hidden unpleasant feeling that he is managing only three people at the time that each of his colleagues are running eight to ten people. Maybe he just wants to feel equal in status and importance to the others regardless of the real load.

Or, when your husband says that he will be happy if you will go out tonight with your friends and he will stay with the kids; that "you really deserve it, in light of the efforts you invest in the family and householding...." And you see—by chance—the schedule on the table that clearly shows that this evening is the broadcast of the basketball game of the team he loves. So, maybe under the "need" of a moral husband who cares for his wife, there is in fact a hidden, personal "want" to see the basketball game without disturbance and interference.

It can be entertaining, but it can also be confusing or annoying.

The third pair of eyeglasses: the "exist"

In the common language, the expression "It is what it is," is the way to emphasize to everybody the need to meet and not deny or ignore the facts. Although recognition of the facts, **"The exists,"** is an important and necessary stage in any situation, the path to continuous recognition includes many obstacles. Most of them stem from the fact that at the same time, reality is also observed from the point of view of the "necessary" and "want-desirable" glasses.

For example: the athlete who spends nights and days practicing while his competitors do much less. The athlete that was sure that he would win the first place by a considerable margin of his competitors because he "deserved it" being as he invested the most. (He sees the "need," the moral aspect that brought him to think and expect that athletes who invest should be rewarded and the idle punished or at the least not recognized). The athlete, who has already seen himself on the podium winning and getting the admiration he so desired (a "want," a wishful way of expectation of someone to whom recognition, appreciation and perhaps also prize money is important) could not stand and accept the "existence" of the fact that he came in third. He became so hurt and insulted—so depressed, that he left races and sports forever.

Let's put things in order!

Everybody uses the three eyeglasses, sometimes together and sometimes separately. But, when we need to start exercising common sense, we need to use them correctly, otherwise there is no chance of an effective solution.

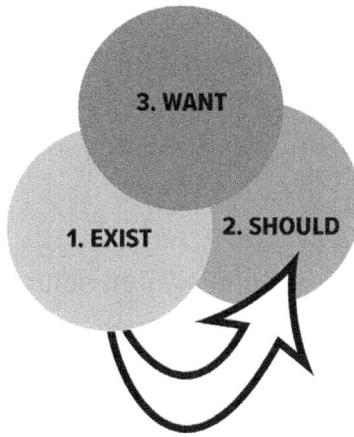

An efficient process of collecting information must bring all those involved—the information collectors and the information providers—to act through a correct process; an order that generates full identification and separation among the existing situation or will ,the wanted will or the should be . As the common saying goes: "What I have… I never wanted, and what I wanted… I never had." However, in life, as the illustration shows, there will always be a zone of overlap, the area in which we are really satisfied (the overlap of the three categories), the area that we are asked or want to change. The problems lie, of course, in the areas of the gaps—the difference and none overlap among should, exist and want. In order to make the right decisions, we have to adopt some rules of traffic in the "square" above.

1. Never begin the process of collecting information and clarifying while using the "want- desire" eyeglasses.

They are important and are a part of the whole picture, they reflect interests, *but* it will be much easier for us to refer to them with the right weight and in the proper context if we have sufficient knowledge and understanding regarding what exists and what is perceived as necessity.

2. Any discussion of an intelligent solution due to a malfunction, problem, event, or even future plans and goals versus reality, require:

    a. Mapping and creating understanding and consensus on the facts. (There are a lot of cases where even the mere efforts to agree on what seem to be simple and clear issues, present problematic and sometimes opposing views.)

    b. Achieving agreement what is defined and means proper and is the correct standard that satisfies or is agreed upon as the should be solution.

    c. Clarify how far the existing situation is in comparison to the should be situation. (Which was the normal, correct, existing situation that has changed or is the goal we decided to achieve).

    d. Planning the solution: Locating, analyzing, handling the problems and supporting the factors with reaching the needed objective.

An illustration that will simplify adapting and adopting traffic laws

My social security agent explained to me how important it is to save a pension that will, in the future, enable me to maintain the standard of living that I am used to. He took out a financial planning form, and after countless questions about my life habits and consumption, came to the conclusion that I would need to save 10,000$ per month. That means that in order to be able to live on an interest rate of 10,000$ per month, I have to create a fund of about 1,000,000$ during the remaining five years until I retire. All that means that I have to set aside 200,000$ each year out of my disposable income, or in monthly saving terms, 17000$--which, of course, I do not have. The agent, quite clearly, did not manage to make a sale. He *did* manage to make me feel miserable. I realized that in addition to the understanding that I was unable to create that sum of a pension, I should keep watching my health and avoid any chance of meeting somebody that will force me to look in the eyes of the future, so to say.

Now, I have an appointment with my will—trying to decide to change habits and lifestyle choices in the hopes of saving more for the future by reducing current expanses.

Dear agent! Always start from the existing reality, and then look on what is needed. The defined need will be built as a realistic and achievable necessity, taking into account all constrains, and checking what can be changed in order to achieve it.

Norman, my dear friend, I feel strongly that I must apologize that I was not sensitive enough when I innocently asked whether you were looking for a lover, and even dared to assume that you probably were. I did not imagine that while I was trying to develop the "wish" of your fantasias, you were already stuck in this "very existing" situation, looking for a way to get out of it so you would be free from her.

How could an understanding be achieved between us, when I speak about "want " and expect an answer from your "desire," in the time that you cannot bear any theoretical discussions about such desires, and you are tuned to receive and understand it as if it relates to your very contemporary and real life? And then, unable to free yourself, you expose yourself and answer the "wish."

Dear Norman, I learned my lesson. I hope that you will read this chapter. I am sure that adopting the traffic rules I have presented here will avoid any chance of creating a malfunction or misunderstanding. You shut yourself up, feeling threatened, hurt, resentful and even ready to disconnect our relationship. I apologize again.

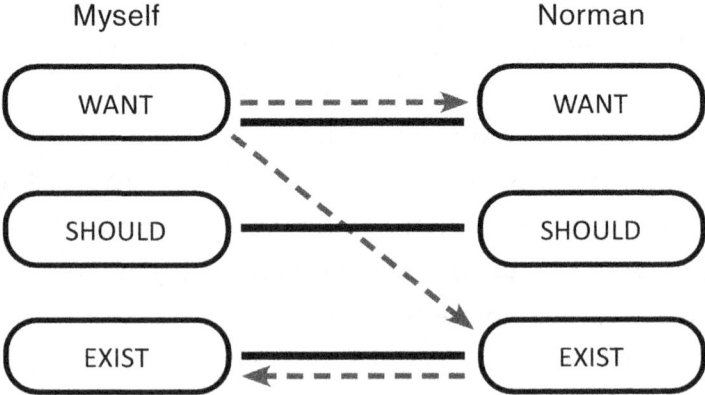

Speak to each other through the same glasses.

Announce and clarify when you switch to another eyeglass.

To speak to someone from one eyeglass when he is tuned to receive and answer from another eyeglass and perspective, is a recipe for failure.

Let's check what happens when the child claims, "I've been with the iPhone for two years now," and the father replies, "Fine, I'm glad you are happy." The boy then falls silent. The fact that he has had the phone for two years is something on which they both will most likely agree. However, in the meaning and implications of the fact, there are enormous gaps. The boy actually wants the iPhone 6. Dad does not think (or does not feel) that the boy needs or wants it. There is no doubt that identifying and speaking openly, and from the same eyeglass—some reference regarding which eyeglass the sentence was said in would facilitate understanding, though not necessarily agreement. For example, the father's answer could be: "You may want to change the phone, but I do not think it is necessary. You do not use most of the functions on your existing device."

Identifying the pair of glasses we wear is important, also when we meet ourselves. It prevents us from manipulating ourselves. For example, when my wife stands at the front of an open, crowded closet and says "I have nothing to wear!" is she aware of that fact that she actually does not want the **existing** (dozens of dresses), and wants to buy a new garment? Or, when she says "I have nothing to wear for this wedding," is she aware of that she is acting from the "need" and the cultural pressure of not to showing up twice around the same family members with the same garment or with a garment that is not new ? Indeed, life is not a garden of roses. .

Now, we can agree with ourselves and our surroundings and say that if you really want to solve something using your common sense, then it's a good idea to gather and organize information; to examine in *addition* to the cold data the manner in which it was presented, the significance and meaning that is attributed to it, and the initial intention for the conversation: the "pair of glasses".

Exercise 2:

Step 1: "catch" and record in writing typical events you have had or that are currently happening to you, including:

1. You felt that your attitude and intention was misunderstood by others.
2. You felt that you were unsure whether you understood the other people's point of view.

Step 2. Record in what way you think you made a mistake or how you have been misunderstood.

Step 3. Build an alternative sentence that has the potential to minimize the chance of misunderstanding.

Step 4. Practice on analyzing yourself to improve effective use in other similar events.

Note: if there is a chance of collaborated practicing with mutual feedback, use it.

At the beginning, you should practice this many times with your colleagues at work, your family and friends. This is assumed to be a more protected environment where you have the opportunity to get constructive feedback to correct a misunderstanding. Later, you can practice putting yourself in situations that require a more synchronized conversation with strangers.

Assuming that the first synchronization is done and the connection and communication between you and your environment and everybody is on the same plane (exist or need or want), and everyone agrees that in order to solve problems we have to work in the systematic order we presented in the traffic cycle, the next step is to learn how to collect data and create a whole and correct picture.

THE INFORMATION FOR GETTING THE WHOLE PICTURE

When you talk to:

A mechanic: They will ask you what was broken or eroded or released.

A device or toolmaker expert: They will ask you from where the command was sent and what was its format?

Metal worker: They will ask where the iron frame is rusted and what point to strengthen?

A beautician: They will explain to you that the material that the colleague gave is not particularly helpful.

A chemist: They will check if the structure of the molecules changed after the catalytic activation.

Psychologist: They will ask who annoyed you.

The computer person: They will say that they did not correctly define the operation of the function.

If you have ever experienced a meeting where everyone talks together about the same problem, you surely and immediately discovered that there is no chance of creating a common database that relates to the whole range of factors that affect the problem. Each expert is focused differently according to his "professional and specialized expertise.

There is a lack of intellect, neutral and unifying, which will deal with the creation of a complete and understandable picture.

What questions we need to ask to get the whole picture?

When you talk with doctors:
Orthopedist: Will ask what is broken or eroded or released?

Neurologist: Will check what nerve receives commands and what is the form of the command.

Surgeon: Will cut the needed point and then sew it up again.

Internal: Will check the molecules and fats in the blood.

Cardiologist: Will check the "pump" pressure and how many times in a minute it draws.

Are the two sections above alike? It turns out, that yes!

We see that there is a similarity between an orthopedist's way of thinking and that of a mechanic, a surgeon and a metal man, the tool maker and the neurologist. Similarity that is expressed in the way of collecting narrow and specific information based on language and specialization.

Here too, in the medical world. There is a little chance of creating a complete picture of the patient's situation and the interrelations between the different systems in his body. We will be able to increase the chance of getting the whole picture when and if we shall ask a general practitioner to "join the club." Hopefully, he will be able to guide a systematic collection of the information, using a unifying language and overcoming the different focus on the attitude of each professional.

It is worth noting than in both cases there are similar phenomena.

The cosmetician and the internal doctor look at the structure of the **material**.

The mechanic and cardiologist both focus on the engine/heart – the **equipment.**

The psychologist and the general practitioner will look and check the **person.**

Did each of the professionals think that they have collected partial and only little information because they asked only one-dimensional questions that were focused on his discipline of expertise?

Has anyone fallen into a circle of doubt regarding the failures in diagnosis and treatment given in light of the fact that it was a one-dimensional way of thinking that relates to one drawer out of the four?

The duty of referring to the four drawers:

The obvious conclusion is the need to decide to accustom ourselves to use **the principle of collecting information in order to feel the four drawers!**

It is important to examine ourselves and identify in which area we are usually more focused, then train ourselves to be ready to gather information in *other* areas that we are less accustomed to relate. If we do not act according to this principle, there is a probability that we will not understand most of the meaning and influence (either damage or benefit) of an event or phenomenon.

Material

A Person

Equipment/Tool

Method/Proccess

For example, after the nurse in the clinic drew my blood, I discovered a blue bruise of blood, under my skin. Although, I, like most of us, tend to think that a failure or a malfunction was created only by one factor, the reality is completely different!!

> **A phenomenon that appears to be one major problem is often made up from several faults and factors that have come together! In many cases, these are mutual influences between the factors, not merely cumulative effects.**

I asked myself why the taking of blood this time went wrong and left me with bruises. I realized that I had to get four kinds of answers before I could try to assume what happened, and what I need to watch or even avoid in the future. All of us have a precondition before attempting to reach any conclusion.

Material. Maybe thicker or thinner blood than in the past. What was the measured blood pressure?

Person. Who was the nurse? New? Old? Nervous? Relaxed?

Equipment. Maybe the needle was not the right one? Was the blade broken? Or alternatively, was the tourniquet weak?

Method. Did she stick the needle right? Did she release the rubber block before time?

I know we can always think that one component, in this case the nurse, is responsible for everything. But, did we think correctly? Were we aware of the fact that at least one more ingredient, the material—the blood—could not be controlled, nor recognized as problem until the moment of the blood test? So, is it not right to think that if we would change either the nurse, needle, or the tourniquet, the bruise could have been avoided?

It is useful to run a systematic questioning process when there is lack of data. (For example, Information about the blood density that we shall have only after we get the test results.

> **The more information we have in all the drawers, the more we will be able to define and understand the meaning and substance of the problem.**
>
> **During the next steps, it will help us to find the causes of the phenomenon, and as a result, find a solution!**

Finding that the needle is correct and appropriate and / or that the rubber blocker was correctly applied, is as important as detecting the defect. The discovery reduces the number of factors that could potentially cause the phenomenon.

I suppose that during the study of the example, you were wondering how this story relates to the way of using our common sense? Do we need to invest all of our time and energy in every phenomenon or action? Perhaps it is simply better to continue with our routine, to live with the problems or even ignore them? Or, in other words, we should meet and decide about the two major questions we should ask:

Is it necessary to treat every problem or malfunction we encounter?

Does everything that happen hold a need to be investigated and\or solved?

The answer is no. you do not have to treat every phenomenon, but it is strongly recommended that we try to diagnose it. We must apply the principles and tools that common sense provides because the price of a double error of taking care of what you do not need and at the same time avoiding dealing with what you need... believe me. It is a truly high and unnecessary price.

One can be more stringent and ask whether it is necessary to invest in collecting and analyzing preliminary information by using all four drawers regarding the cases we do not intend to handle? The answer is that in the absence of preliminary information, the decision will be more emotional and hold less mental consideration and judgment. This will be accompanied with unconscious risk taking that were not exposed to beforehand. Therefore, the right move is that only after getting the initial information and analyzing it can we make an effective **situational decision** that determines what we intend to do or not do with the phenomenon. We expect that the initial analysis will bring us from a bank of facts that seem to be disconnected and without mutual influence to an upgraded insight in which we try to gain more understanding of the connections and mutual influences between the four components: people, material, equipment and methods and about the impact of the situation

For example: the recipe book that my mother got from my grandmother that included the recipe of how to make dumplings. A recipe that included a "trap" that caused the fact that my mother made them "just fine," and my grandmother's were always "excellent."

A perennial study in both of their kitchens revealed that although they would use the same oven(equipment), used the same material, pour the dough in the same way, there was a difference in the final product. It turned out that the instructions on how to cook in hot water that my mother got were far from accurate.

While my mother put the dumplings in the pan while the water was heating up, my grandmother waited until the water was boiling and then dropped them in the pan for a high and immediate heat stroke. Now, it is clear to us that there was some difference in the method and processes of preparation. A difference that my grandmother didn't dare to expose or share, with the intention of winning all the appreciation again and again!

Let's go back to my elevator event and try to figure out if there was a possibility to improve my treatment of it and shorten the time that I had been inside the elevator.

If, before I started to the receptionist (and I give him much credit), I would have thought about how to build the communication so that he could rescue me as soon as possible, or in other words: to "put myself in his shoes," inside his perception of reality, and from there to lead him to share and feel *my* reality, too.

People: failures and malfunctions are relatively rare events for the information and security man during his daily activities.

The equipment: There are control screens with a status chart and warning lights for each elevator. From his position, the man cannot see the entrance of each of the nine elevators.

The method: from the perspective of the reception man, reality is mainly the signs that appear in the control system and not what actually happens. He saw a disabled **elevator** that was shut down for **maintenance and eight elevators that were in normal condition.**

Material: the information he receives from various sources. (Telephone bell, users, technicians). The ringing bell tells him that that someone is stuck, but he does not know in which elevator and on what floor. He comes again to the same conclusion when the emergency bell from inside the elevator rings. Still, he does not know which elevator to associate that with, and that everything is presented as okay except one elevator that probably has no one in it because there are warning signs not to enter it.

There is a mental barrier that the security man ought to pass before using the systematic and logical seven steps process that is shown in the table below. the rational understanding that it is a mistake to have 100 % confidence in the electronic diagnostic system that is built on the control screens and ignore physical observation.

THE SEVEN STEPS PROCESS

The seven steps process

7. Preventing a chance of the problem returning.

6. Select the applicable solution and its implementation.

5. Find possible solutions.

4. Analysis and detection of factors.

3. Mapping all components of the event or failure.

2. Making a situational decision.

1 . Watchfulness and giving meaning to the existing information.

SITUATIONAL DECISION MAKING

If and how to deal with the phenomenon we identified.
Sometimes, the decision is made in fractions of a second,
combining an instinctive response with a quick analysis of
the situation.

When the fluorescent lamp starts to fall on the head of
your friend sitting next to you, you are likely to quickly push
him aside and shout. You probably did not have time to plan
whether he would fall off the chair or not. You decided to
deal with the immediate danger.

Sometimes, the situation is reversed, and we do not treat
or handle the problem.

For example: when you discovered that the tap in the
shower was dripping every few seconds, did you immediately change the rubber bands and fix it? Or has it been
dripping for years and you'd simply become accustomed
to the noise?

These two non-coincidental examples were brought to
present the fact that we do not tend to distinguish between
immediacy and importance, and a lot of time mix them
together in our decisions.

What is important is not necessarily immediate
What is immediate is not necessarily important
necessarily important.

Important and not immediate Plan when you will handle and how much time you will spend on it.	**Immediate and important** Handle immediately. Use the maximum time and energy needed.
Not immediate, unimportant Postpone but keep in periodic control.	**Immediate. Unimport-ant** Handle immidiatly with minimum time and resources

The degree of damage or benefit that the phenomenon causes or will cause. Important--

Immediately – means execution as soon as possible.

For example, there is a good chance that if you did not clearly put into your calendar when you have to do the annual vehicle licensing test, you'd find yourself urgently canceling other appointments and running at the last day—or even the day afterwards—to do the test. Because now, the annual test have left the category of "important but not immediate" and moved to the urgent category which means" important and immediate". It is accumulating urgency without any awareness on our part.

I am also not cruel enough to ask you when you plan on treating the sensitivity to cold or heat that you discovered in your tooth?

By the way, even the leak of the tap that appears at the moment and is interpreted neither important nor immediate, can change its status and eventually become an increasing flow that will call for an urgent treatment.

The inevitable conclusion is that it is not enough to ask whether the phenomenon is important or immediate. In order to make the right decision whether to handle it or not, there are two more answers that we owe to ourselves.

First, do we have control over the phenomenon?

Second, is the phenomenon singular, or does it recur in some cycle; is it constant and continuous?

Attaining control over a phenomenon or situation and the familiarity and ability to predict the cyclicality brings us (even the adventurous among us) to calm down, which enables us to focus our activities on planned and initiative and ongoing activities.

Take a look for example how relaxed you are when you find yourself at the same place and at the same time in the traffic jam on your daily way to work. Much calmer than a surprise jam that you have no prediction of its duration or length.

The situation of "positive boredom" is really so joyful that we tend to allow ourselves to plan more surprises and adventures.

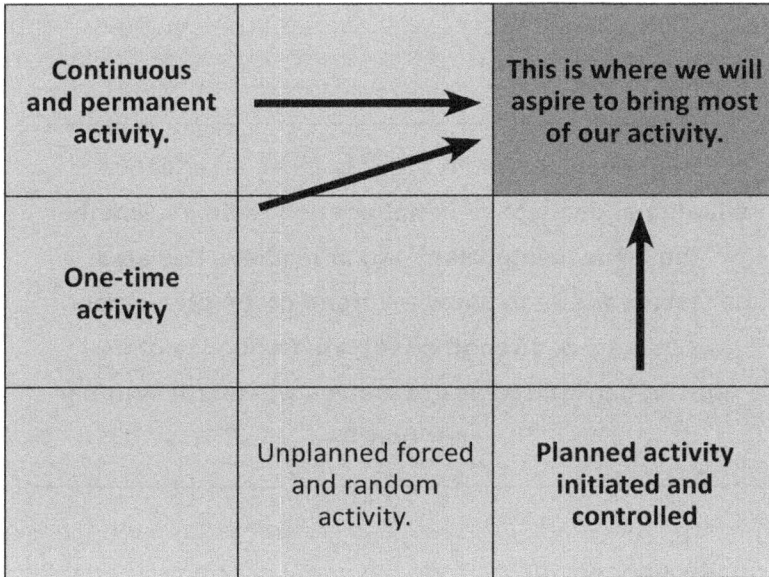

Continuous and permanent activity.	→	**This is where we will aspire to bring most of our activity.**
One-time activity		↑
	Unplanned forced and random activity.	**Planned activity initiated and controlled**

Let's remember the annual car test. It's known, and if it's planned, it comes back every year.

Why do we not get used to a habit of renewing it before the deadline? instead of pressure of last moment, we'll do it three weeks earlier, actually calm.

The pain in your tooth—Is this a recurring malfunction? Yes! If not in the same tooth, then in another one, perhaps? Is the pain rate increasing? No! So if that's the case, then it should be that the situational decision will be to treat the aching tooth immediately before it becomes an urgent problem where we lose the ability to control it.

And what about the other teeth? Do you intend to do preventive treatment? Something that means a planned activity, expressed in regular and periodic activity of the dentist's semi-annual treatment (I do not get a percentage of his salary).

> **We conclude that in order to make an effective situational decision, it is not enough to define whether the issue is important and immediate. It is also necessary for us to know the trend of the phenomenon (weakened, strengthened), the frequency of its appearance, and to ask ourselves whether it is under our control**

And the innocent tap? Do we have any information or ability to control the rate of escalation?

And if not, and if we postponed time after time, we should do ourselves a favor and put it in constant surveillance, so it would not surprise us when its status changes! A process whose practical meaning is to try from time to time to shut the water tap at the entrance to the apartment to see that it is not stuck.

Anyone who is angry at himself because he answers e-mails and texts all the time, a forced and ongoing phenomenon, must ask himself what to do in order to free himself and devote time to what is really important to him—something planned. It will not come to this if he does not (at least partially) gain control over the repetitive randomness. **Planned and proactive action of media handling is preferable to reacting activity.**

Now, after we have collected preliminary information about the phenomenon, the problem, the deviation from the normal and predictable, we are ready to ask ourselves:

What types of situational decisions can make, and which are preferable?

In each decision there is a need to define the gap between the situation in which we want to be and the existing situation. This is the target for our solution process activity!

Let's look at several possible types of situational decisions:

Acceptance of the situation:
Seventy-year-old Joshua used to walk up three flights of stairs with wide strides, including two stairs at a step. Lately, he has found that the action causes panting, and has had to go up one stair at a time. He has to stop at the stairwell to catch his breath after every half floor. It does not seem to him that it is desirable or possible to make an effort to return to the past, so he adapts and tries to accept the new situation.

Delay in handling.

Shirley saw on her phone that the battery was weak, even though she'd barely spoken that day, but she "had to" make a few more calls to invite her friends to the spontaneous pajama party she wanted to do that night. She could not make the last call because the phone was off and there was no charger or electrical socket near her. Well, one less pajama-party member.

Repair and return to standard and familiar mode.

Michael looked desperately at the slowness (which he was unaccustomed to) of the speed that the sites were uploading on the computer screen. He was even startled to find out that he was working at 5 megabits instead of the 25 he was paying for. From that moment on, "there was no one to talk to." He decided that the problem would be solved, even if he had to spend the night on the line with the service people of the communications company.

Upgrade and develop to a new standard.

At the collector's car show, Joseph saw how the Alpha Spider that was owed by his friend was accelerating much faster than his own Alpha. While drinking coffee, Alfred shared with him that he improved performance by putting an electronic fuel injector instead of the mechanical pump that is standard.

I suppose it is clear to the readers that Joseph, who is traveling with the Alpha just like before, feels miserable and will likely make every effort to assemble such an injector into his own car. What was at the beginning nothing but a possible upgrade, became a new standard Joseph truly wants to reach.

> **It is worth remembering that in life we meet with many kinds of phenomena and mishaps. Therefore, you should be alert and ready to make decisions at any moment! Should you...**
>
> **Accept the change? * postpone the contest? ***
>
> ***repair and revert to previous state? * Upgrade to the desired purpose?**

The happiest among us, who have gained control over their lives, can even plan when they will make decisions about upgrading and improving their status (car, home, wife, husband, career, hobby, cat... etc.).

To you who meets forced changes that land on you without warning, I highly recommend (If possible), to create a pause between the decision-making stage, which defines where and how we want to be, and the diagnostic processes: the activities and decisions that will follow. There are situations during which we deal immediately. There are other situations that the time is ripe to deal with them, and it is worthwhile to define priorities for them in planning the time, means and attention we invest.

Let us summarize the main steps for determining a reference to a phenomenon or problem. Assuming that we have collected the information according to what I have proposed so far:

1. We will try to break up the big problem into its components. In most cases, there were a Number of smaller faults that joined together to create the big fault.

For example, it is impossible to save a substantial amount of money on "family expenses." But you can decide to turn off unnecessary lights to save power. You can also decide to unify different tasks, such as (shopping, mail, bank, work) and reduce the number of trips and fuel consumption. **Most of us have a better ability to deal with smaller things and maybe simpler ones, too, rather than something big and unfortunately also complex.**

2. We will define the priority of treatment according to the principles of importance, immediacy, and the measure of control that we have on the phenomenon and its effects.

For example: In storage facilities, around large fuel tanks, there are collecting pools that have been built up larger than the volume of the tank. Pools where the fuel is expected to leak in case of a failing tank—an area that is planned and ready to prevent or at least reduce the damage. A system that is prepared to provide an effective answer in case we cannot prevent the emergence of the malfunction.

3. We shall set the boundaries and areas of treatment of the phenomenon, in accordance with the determination of the situational decision.

For example: your neighbor is drumming drastically at 02:00 am and you cannot sleep or even try to ignore it. It is highly recommended you should decide in advance what is the limit of your intervention. (Contacting the police, telephone, knock on the door, setting up a counter noise, breaking into the house and destroying the drums?)

It is usually important to stick to the "what"—in this case achieving quiet. But one must not forget to try to choose the right "how". It is possible that by choosing the wrong way of acting you could achieve immediate silence, but also hostility and future confrontation with the neighbor.

4. Define the limits of ability and responsibility.

If the ability to solve the problem lies beyond your control, your means, or your professionalism, try to recruit the relevant missing means. Most of the time, the higher price is the cheaper one.

For example: a cyclist is hit by a vehicle and lies still on the road. Is it right to move him off the road and perhaps create more damage (because you are not a professional), or perhaps the better decision would be to call an ambulance and try to prevent the man from being hit by another vehicle.

5. We should plan the treatment of the problem with attention and careful activities in order to not cause any further problems or damage during the process.

For example: You better consider the situation carefully before taking a strong pill against headaches (which causes some drowsiness) before trying to drive to your home while "relaxed". You may find yourself taken to hospital after the pill has done a "good job" (as it was expected to do) after you woke up from your deep sleep in the middle of the shop's window, stuck in a cake.

> **Please remember! In some cases, it is particularly important to gain control of the phenomena in order to prevent further damage and malfunctions during the diagnosis, treatment, and implementation of the solution.**
>
> **Control and prevention of damage can be achieved by:**
>
> **1. Isolating the phenomenon from its surrounding.**
>
> **2. Attempt to prevent the environment from affecting the problem**

Typical examples from different worlds:

From the world of electricity: We all expect that when installing a new fuse on the power board, we will stop the voltage to the board by using a switch between us and the supply net for the safety of the installer.

It is done to prevent a short from a live wire that will cause more damage or even flat out kill the installer. We isolated the board from its environment.

From the medical world: We all expect that the operating room will be sterile, and that the patient and the surgical area will not be affected by the bacterial army that was waiting to contaminate and injure even more than the original problem.

From the fire world: In a forest fire, surface clearance is performed so that the fire will burn only a defined area.

We isolated the burning part of the forest. We would be happy to find out that the foresters have done a preventive action by keeping cleared areas permanently so. It enables preventing, or at least minimizing, future damages when the fire begins. Let us treat in the present the expected problems that can appear in the future.

And in banking: The bank gives a credit framework to the customer in one hand, and builds a software border to block the ability to take more money than the frame. The bank has defined in advance the limit of the damage that the customer can make. The bank has isolated your activity from the other financial activities.

Now is the right moment to create the needed distinction between malfunction and risk.

RISK.	FAULT.
A threat that in the future something will go wrong and change from a normal situation to a problem or fault.	Deviation from a normal situation that happened in the past. A deviation that can exist in the present and escalate in the future.

Future   **Present**   **Past**

DIAGNOSIS AND ITS TOOLS

After we decided that:

1. We are treating the phenomenon or problem/fault.
2. When we will treat it.
3. With whom.
4. What is the proper state we want to reach.

We will begin using tools that will help our common sense to make much better diagnostics of the causes of problems or malfunctions that we want to repair, and bring it back to a normal situation. Our first attempt will be to try to **identify the causes** that created the phenomena that we were aware of at the first stage.

It is important to distinguish between a symptom and a cause.

SYMPTOM.	FACTOR.
The phenomenon that is identified, seen, and felt as a result of an event or factor, that treating it will not bring to any solution.	The entity/substance that caused the event. When it will be identified and corrected, everything will return to normal.

Please be aware of the fact that in many cases, the essence that is perceived as a factor is itself a symptom of a primary and earlier factor. Therefore, our diagnostic process will make any attempt to approach and get the primary cause of the chain.

For example, would you agree with the following statement (written when some of the cities are flooded with water)?

The lack of washing and cleaning the high voltage isolation elements on the high voltage lines from the dust of the sandstorms flooded the cities.

It seems that there is no connection... but!

- The rain and the strong winds formed shorts and cut off electrical lines because of not washing off the dust.
- In order to access the lines for repairs, the tree branches were cut and left in the streets with the intention to collect them.

- Another rain swept the leaves and chaff into the draining holes and filled some of them.
- The drainage channels that had not been cleaned before winter were partially blocked.
- The rainwater that was not drained flooded the streets.

I suppose that you would agree that if the insulators were washed, there would have been no shortcuts in the electrical system. Then, you would not have had to cut the wood, nor would you have pruned... The drain wouldn't have been blocked... And, there wouldn't have been flooding!

But maybe we tend to refer to the symptom? Stormy winds and heavy rain during the fall would bring the same results, even without the electrical faults. Perhaps the primary and main factors lie with the drainage planning, which was not built for such quantities of water, or perhaps because it was planned for clear water and not a stream of mud, or perhaps even the lack of preventive cleaning before the rainy season which prevented maximum capacity of the system?

It's convenient to blame the electricity company and at the same time to "forget" to put the focus on the municipal authorities.

From this example we can learn that if each had contributed his functional and professional ability to the preventive treatment in time, a considerable part, or even *all* the phenomena that were brought about in this chain of events, would have been avoided or at least reduced in intensity and damage.

All of us can adopt the conclusion that:

In some cases, it is sufficient to identify and treat the cause (even if it is an intermediate factor), which, with its correction, will restore the system to its normal functioning! And here, it depends very much on who we are and how we relate to the phenomenon or malfunction or risk.

For example- a typical phenomenon in our visits to a doctor:

Ronaldo came to the doctor and told him that his head was "exploding in pain". After finding nothing during the preliminary effort to diagnose the problem, the doctor decided to give him a pill to relieve the pain.

The doctor is aware of the fact that he merely treated the symptom (the headache) and that he returned Ronaldo to temporary correctness, something which will pass when the effect of the pill will begin to reduce. Ronaldo will probably have to come to the clinic several times until the doctor will become despaired of repeating the previous treatment and decide to send Ronaldo to do extensive tests. After the tests, it was found that Ronaldo had gastric problems that caused the headaches. So, now we have to check and treat the stomach.

After the stomach was checked, it was discovered that Ronaldo had a liver problem. When the doctor asked himself from where the problem came, he concluded that the source lay in the bottle of whisky that Ronaldo sipped at almost daily. When the doctor asked Ronaldo why he drank so much, he answered that "it is heritage from home, my father and grandfather drank a lot". We have no choice but to come to the conclusion that Ronaldo's grandfather, who has not been alive for many years, was the actual cause for Ronaldo's headaches!

It is recommended to learn that it is not always necessary to reach and treat the primary factor, which in this case is to make Ronaldo's grandfather stop drinking in heaven. Ronaldo will not see it, and therefore he will not be affected! It's enough to make Ronaldo stop drinking whisky in order to prevent the "explosive headaches!"

> **The first effort that we have to do as a result of the collected information is to try to identify the cause or causes of the phenomena.**

Success in this effort leads to **redefinition of the subject to treatment.**

Instead of treatment, headache prevention will take care of not drinking whisky.

> **The first stage we took led us to: Resetting and redefining the problem we intend to solve**

Before looking at the logic of an effective diagnostic process that identifies the causes of the faults, and therefore the possibilities for correction and resolution, it is important to be aware of the fact that the diagnostic process itself can "complicate life" by changing the reality that is examined by creating additional faults, amplifying , weakening or even eliminating the problem (the worrying part is the temporary disappearance of a malfunction and its appearance again at an unknown time). Therefore, common sense recommends planning a gradual diagnostic process which will begin from little to stronger intervention.

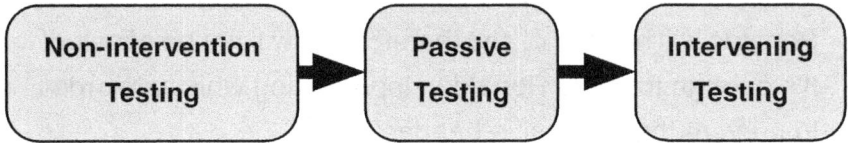

| Non-intervention Testing | → | Passive Testing | → | Intervening Testing |

To illustrate: when the light bulb stops working, most of us assume it burned. The typical operation is screwing it out and replacing it with another one. If the new one works, the old one is thrown away. Maybe you threw away a normal lamp which was not screwed in deeply enough? If the new bulb also doesn't turn on, some of us will try a third. If it does turn on, is it possible that we now have two bulbs that we do not know whether they are burned or not?

The reason is that we probably did not control the number of screw spins and maybe only the third lamp was screwed deep enough.

There is also a possibility that we will take an electric testing screwdriver to touch the contacts and make sure if there is electrical supply (the light in the screwdriver will turn on if there is).It will give us information that the voltage reaches the lamp house and will focus us on the bulbs themselves. This is, of course, conditioned to being careful enough not to create another malfunction by making a short between the two contacts in the lamp with the screwdriver. If this happens, then even the lamp house is damaged, and perhaps the fuse in the electrical control board will be burned.

According to my experience only a few of us will make an effort to conduct an uninterrupted test by looking through the side of the lamp to see if the fiery wire is torn or not. A test that supplies more information without creating more mishaps!

Another illustration: Steve, the owner of Banana Packing House, decided one day to check how many crates his workers fill in an hour in order to try to improve the packaging speed because he suspected that his weekly average was low. He came every hour and counted the packed crates. Surprisingly, while he was at the packing house and did the registration, the result was satisfactory. The pace was almost twice as high as the typical daily rate. You, the reader may be smiling… he smiled less. When he got an answer from one of the workers after asking him for the reason of the results, he answered immediately, even without thinking, "that's because you were there and recorded." It means that the test that was seemingly (!) un-interrupting, changed the reality. (In psychology they call it "experimenter effect"). Now he had to look for a way to check the production rate by other means that will assure non-interference. He was also worried that it would show that the staff was working lazily all the times when he was not in the packing house.

This is the time to practice: practicing can lead you to acquire and gain practical ability to use the principles.

Exercise 3:

- Choose one or more of the following events, preferably one that is close to your daily reality where you live and try to elaborate the phenomena in depth to make an effort to generate insights.
- Use everything you've read and learned until now. (Don't hesitate to read the principles again and again).
- When choosing a solution to the event, ask yourself which thinking tool and guiding principles you have used.
- You are invited to practice as much as possible and on a variety of topics. It is beneficial to meet various kinds of problems that bother you in everyday life.

Please follow the recommended steps in each event you have chosen to practice.

1. Try to define the chain of factors that caused the described situation.
2. Assuming that you can handle only one topic, what is the issue you will be addressing to minimize or prevent damage?
3. Assuming that you can act to prevent the happening of the same problem in the future—what would you do?

Event 1: In February, when you conducted the annual report to the tax authorities, you found out that you not only failed to save money, you also reduced your amount of savings from the previous year.

Event 2: What you initially thought was a single case, turned out to be a recurring phenomenon. For several months, your husband/wife has been making every possible effort not to go out with your best friends.

Event 3: the forecaster warned of a snowstorm and cold weather the next day. You decided to check the maximum warming strength of the home heating system that was not activated for long time. You found out that it barely works.

Event 4: your adolescent child begins to tell you about all kinds of new friends, but he does not share too many details. At the same time, he comes home every night a little later then the night before. You do not know how to interpret the change.

Recommendations for further practice:

- Find more problems or issues from your life that last for a long time. Apply the same pattern of thinking towards them in order to identify the most primary cause of the chin of factors and the factor that it's treatment will bring a significant in the situation.
- If you have a friend or even a group of friends who are willing to read, discuss and even practice all the exercises in the book with you, it can be productive and beneficial for each one.

Thinking recommendation : please activate two questions at the minute that you assume that you have reached the initial end of the chain of factors.

1. Why and how the cause was formed?
2. Is there an ability to identify an earlier factor in the chain that caused the factors that we have identified. Please remember the example of Ronaldo's grandfather's headache and alcohol.

THE 5-7 STEPS CHAIN OF WHYS

Ask why- get an answer- ask again why about the considerations and logic that led to the answer- get the second answer- ask again why about consideration and logic of the second answer-get the third answer. and so on. After 5-7 chains, you will find out that you will reach previous factors that are the sources of the factors that lead to the phenomenon that appears to be the source of the problem.

Now let's be perfect!

Let us return to the definition of the phenomenon, the problem, the fault.
This time we will ask what kind of information we should gather?

SOLUTION-MAKING DECISION

It is important to remember that during the first stage of collecting information, we defined **the principle of the four drawers,** that invites common sense to ask questions about four different subjects in order to get the complete picture of a phenomenon: **People, method**, **equipment and material** (I hope there is no need to refresh your memory by running after you with the syringe needle of the blood test...)

Let's put the four drawers on hold and get into improving the use of our common sense, specifically, learning and getting acquainted with another set of questions that will increase our understanding and ability as to how to locate the factors. The next step will be connecting the four drawers and the set of questions and creating a very **practical and useful tool to locate factors, analyze them, and find solutions to problems in all areas of life.**

Attention! Even if the next step seems a bit complicated, do not give up! Your effort will be beneficial. Everything will be clear and understood and you will have **an effective tool that will serve you all your life—in all its aspects!**

Let's deal a little bit with family gossip:

Shulamit and Steve hang out in the same social circles as Rebecca and Max. Steve is always wondering why his wife is so nice and friendly to Max and so aggressive and rude to Rebecca. Steve tried again and again to ask Shulamit about her feelings toward Rebecca and also to check whether Rebecca did anything wrong to her. The answer was really surprising. Shulamit insisted that she respects Rebecca very much and that Rebecca had never done anything wrong to her! Steve called me desperately and asked me for advice. He wanted to know what to ask in order to understand what was going on and to be able to avoid tension and "explosions" in the future. Steve made it clear that he has no intention of giving up the company of Rebecca and Max.

I strongly suggested to use the following **five dimensions,** expressing my confidence that they will surely help **to define the problem!**

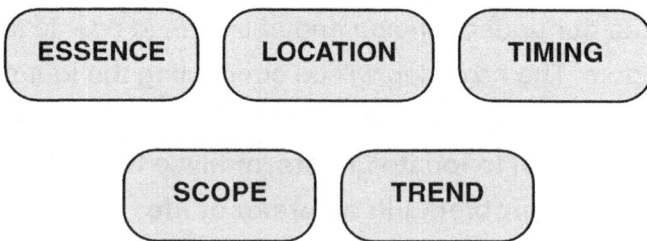

ESSENCE	LOCATION	TIMING

SCOPE	TREND

I added that gathering information about each dimension would significantly increase the chance that we will be able to have a firm understanding regarding the whole picture and thus enable us to solve it, or at least decrease its damage. I also brought to his attention that perhaps the apparent aggression was a symptom of other factors that were as of yet unknown.

Steve stared at me confusedly and said that he had no idea how to connect the five dimensions with his wife, then definitely not to function systematically and have them create some kind of a diagnostic process.

I smiled and said that a systematic process is sometimes a bit boring, but by consistently using systematic thinking without involving feelings, leads to finding the real factors that caused the phenomenon. We even made a simulation how to ask for the information in practice.

Essence	What	What: happened, deviation, wrong. What: part, material, person, method of action is the problem?
Location	Where	Where is: the part, material, the spoiled person? Where are the flaws on: part, material, man, data?
Timing	When	When was it noticed first. When did the problem begin? A circumstantial or casual connection.
Scope	How much or many	How much happened, might happen. What size, importance, influence?
Trend	Direction frequency	Increasing, decreasing, stable, cyclical. Identified or unknown.

The information that Steve managed to collect was:

ESSENCE	Shulamit behaves like this only to Rebecca.
IDENTITY	
LOCATION	It happens only when Steve is around
TIMING	It seems to Steve that it began to happen after Ingrid told Shulamit about the frequent quarreling between max and Rebecca. Steve also recalled that before marriage, when Shulamit was a friend of Howard, she behaved similarly to Angelica who was beautiful and charming.
SCOPE	The high level of aggression appears always at the beginning of the evening and after Steve becomes angry and unpleasant and moves away from max and Rebecca. His wife Shulamit then becomes more pleasant to Rebecca.
TREND	It seems to Steve that this behavior has a permanent pattern.

When we met, I asked him if he had any idea about the reasons for Shulamit's behavior towards Rebecca. He smiled sadly and answered with a bit of relief that he does not know yet, but he has an assumption that the problem was not Rebecca, because she had behaved similarly toward Angelica in the past. His thought was that he was not the cause either.

I wonder what else she did not tell him about herself.

Steve also added that when he wandered among the friends in the room and did not stay beside her, there was no agitation, and everything remained calm. During their next meeting with his friends, even when he spoke to Rebecca alone, his wife became engaged and aggressive even when a few seconds before she was listening patiently to other persons. What now? Where is it going? What does she think—That he was prepared to constantly suffer her whims and aggressiveness? That he would agree to her destroying his relationship with his childhood friend?

I had to remind him of the rules of "existing", "wanted" and "necessary" glasses, and suggested to avoid using the "necessary" glasses and use only the "existing" glasses until he was sure he knew and understood all the facts! I expressed the fear that if he behaved differently, he would begin to be angry and hateful toward his wife… which of course created a more difficult problem to solve.

Steve had promised to try. For me, it was a real opportunity to explain to him the practical meaning of avoiding using the "necessary" glasses, at least until all needed information was collected.

Collecting information means collecting facts! With no evaluation and no interpretation!

It is important for Steve and for all of us to learn one more principle: the principle of

No disqualification and non-preference.

A principle that protects us from biases and distorted interpretations based on attitudes and feelings. We must use common sense; we should be careful of the trap of using:

Judgement	This is gross and impolite behavior
Preference	It was better to politely inquire why she was talking to her.
Evaluation	I think Rebecca is afraid of beautiful women.
Disqualification	She could not have behaved like that before. Pity to ask.
Scaling	It is much better for her to be polite than aggressive.

> **Avoiding using the five mechanisms increases the ability to collect unbiased data in a logical and objective way, with a will to accept the facts as they are.**

Steve looked at me and said that he did understand what he was expected **not to do**, but now he was expecting to get an explanation as to **what he actually *should* do**: How to ask the right questions, how to advance in the process of gathering facts and how to build understanding.

At this time, I asked Steve to use the "Funnel Law", and he could not really figure out the connection between a funnel and his wife Shulamit. I asked him if he could put the jealousy aside for a moment and try to understand what common sense did with a funnel. Steve smiled and said that he did not believe that events could be brought into a funnel, but he was willing to try. We agreed that we would first learn and know how the funnel functioned and then examine our ability to use it.

The funnel is a term for a three-step work process that runs about the same as any funnel in the kitchen. When we squeeze an orange on its grains and content, we pour it into a wide mouth (the principle of non-disqualification and preference is activated at this stage of the process). In the second stage, we separate the juice from the rest of particles, using the strainer inside the funnel. In the third stage, we collect and use the filtered juice that came out of the mouthpiece on the way to the glass.

The same process can be applied to any subject and any kind of stream of information or materials that we intend to analyze in order to reach a solution.

Let's examine, for example, a situation in which you are standing at an airport waiting for a guest who is supposed to exit from the incoming flights. You are likely to agree that the sequence of actions will be the following:

1. Position yourself where you see the incoming stream of passengers (which is an effort to get a complete picture of all those who are coming in with the stream of passengers.)
2. Start a filtering system for those who are entering by using prior information that you have about them. (Their appearance or clothes.) Alternatively, you will put a sign with his name to allow the guest to do the filtering and finding you out of the crowd.
3. Now, after filtering and isolating the visitor out of the others, you can collect him.

The same funnel law works effectively in filtering juice or passengers. I assume that you are convinced that the three stages are relevant to all types of problems, from human to human, business, and to technical issues.

Application of the funnel operation principle.

1. Gathering stage: create a complete picture, as wide as possible, from the collection of the details. At this stage, we will collect everything we can without ruling out anything. We do not know yet to evaluate what is important, favorite, relevant etc., and what is not.

2. Filtration and Elimination: At this stage, the components and the characteristics of the filter will allow filtration and transmission of relevant information that affects or correlates, and the information that does not affect and is irrelevant to analyzing the phenomenon.

> Note: It is suggested that if there are doubts and lack of confidence about the existence level of influence, we should pass on the information and apply further filtering and examination.

3. **Isolation and selective** collection of issues to treat out of the total and determination of the limits of repair, treatment, planning etc.

At this stage we have we have filtered and relevant information which will be the basis for analysis to create insights and identify and understand the cause of the given malfunction or future risks.

The funnel entrance is open wide, and its exit is narrow!

Essence. Location. Timing. Scope. Trend

After agreeing that we must apply to the law of non-disqualification, and hold no early judgment or assessment, we will collect any information as an answer to the dimensions.

Let us look again at the case of Steve and Shulamit. We are going to collect any possible information.

The topics of collection:

Trend—Is Shlomit's behavior: cyclical, steady, growing, weakening?

Location—In which places does the eruption take place and in proximity to whom or why?

Timing—Is the relationship identified in relation to the reciprocal effect in which the behavior appears together with situations, times, events, or certain content?

Essence—What is the meaning, the contents, the repeated interests that are expressed during the outburst?

Scope—Does it happen anytime? Anywhere?

After completing the collection, we will proceed to the screening stage, which aims to define what is relevant, connected or affected by the subject matter and what is not.

In the case of Steve and Shulamit, we will try to examine the existence or non-existence of the influence of physical environment on the existence or nonexistence of the outbursts: The proximity of people, the content of the conversation, etc.

We will mention and emphasize the principle that defines that all information gathering should be done in comparison to standards. Standards that are known, accepted measures that express the normal state of affairs.

In the case of Steve and Shulamit, we will ask ourselves what is accepted to be a normative style of speech and relationship between spouses and among friends.

At the end of screening, we will be able to isolate between the subjects that influence and the subjects that affect the behavior as a consequence of the deviation from normal.

(We will see that Steve is becoming slowly but surely a well-trained user in operating the methodology of common sense and achieving effective solutions).

But, as it happens frequently in life, Steve also has problems with the car which, naturally, is a cause of great frustration.

Our friend Steve came with his car to the garage, claiming that he does not understand why his car consumes a quarter of a gallon every five miles, even though it is expected to make about ten miles per quarter.

Ostensibly, the mechanic has the definition of the extent of the fault, which is the degree of deviation of the existing fuel consumption compared with the producer's standard. But, in fact, the mechanic realized that Steve was referring to the designer's standard which was very different from Steve's car consumption. The designer examined the vehicle under optimum conditions of road quality, quantity and weight of cargo, fuel quality, controlled speed and comfortable weather. The designer did not know the way Steve used his car.

The mechanic was experienced enough to know that

in order to answer Steve it was also necessary to check Steve's way of use. After collecting information about the road where he drove, it turned out to be a steep and long way. So too it seemed that Steve drove everywhere with another 600 pounds of camping equipment. It also became apparent that he refueled at the cheapest and most questionable station in the area. Steve also shared proudly that he becomes annoyed when he is overtaken by others and that he pushes the gas pedal until he is again leading at the front.

After being exposed to all these facts, the mechanic said he was really pleasantly surprised by the fuel consumption! He added that he had nothing to fix and that the car behaved as expected from that model. The mechanic suggested that if Steve really wanted to reduce the consumption he had to:

- Reduce the amount and weight of the cargo.
- Drive at a constant speed without unnecessary slows, stops or accelerations."
- Buying fuel at a reliable station, with higher quality gas.

The mechanic said that only then it would be possible to isolate and see the degree of influence of each factor on fuel consumption (the same principle that was demonstrated during the discussion about saving household expenses).

A malfunction or huge problems usually contain a number of small faults. It is difficult for us to handle and manage big faults. Meeting small problems after isolating them is the easier and more practical way to reach solutions. In any case, the mechanic suggested to Steve to be satisfied if the consumption of his car is similar to the standards of similar cars of the same age and with the same mileage.

> **Remember! It is important to ensure that when you are looking for a deviation from the standard, that all those that are involved know and agree to which standard you refer and want to return to and repair. The planner? The user? The maintainer?**

The skilled mechanic used a principle which can be a philosophy of life! He knew that he could not cope with such a huge problem of excess consumption of 80% fuel per mile. Therefore, he acted according to the principle that guides to break or split a huge problem to the small problems that make it up. It is reasonable because:

> **We know how to handle mishaps and small problems!**

Then, Steve would be able to save 0.1 gallon per mile by loading less baggage. Another 0.1 gallon by changing hid driving style, another 0.1 gallon by using only good-quality fuel. And by adding more air to the tires, he will reduce the contact area with the road and by so doing, reduce friction and fuel consumption.

When Steve almost turned away, the mechanic asked him with a little smile if his wife Shulamit is still aggressive toward Rebecca?

Steve replied with a hesitant smile, that after collecting the information about all five indexes:

> **Essence. Location. Timing. Scope. Trend**

He believes he knows how to redefine the phenomenon, and that according to his understanding, Rebecca was not connected and was not part of the problem, because Shulamit behaved the same way in the past with Angelica. He even added that he assumes that he himself was not connected because Shulamit behaved the same way also with Howard.

Maybe Shulamit's problem is with *Shulamit*?

> **It is valuable to remember that redefining a phenomenon or a malfunction during the progressive process of analyzing and diagnosing.**
>
> **The chance to find a solution to the causes and not to the symptoms is increased.**

The mechanic smiled cheerfully and told Steve that although there was still no diagnosis, Steve correctly used the "funnel law" and the set of questions that apply to all five indicators. It seemed that he had succeeded to isolate the problem.

Steve was more hesitant. He tended to think that the main problem was Rebecca, but maybe there were contributing factors? Maybe something in Rebecca's behavior resembled that of Angelica's and thus Shulamit lost control? Maybe it was him who was doing something similar to Howard's behavior in the past and that was what caused Shulamit's behavior?

Smiling and almost laughing, the mechanic shared his satisfaction from the fact that he deals mainly with cars. A second later, he muttered to himself that he actually has a lot of dealings with the drivers, or sometimes with the quality of fuel. He became sad when the thoughts about the times people damaged cars with indifference.

Suddenly, his eyes lit up and he said to Steve, "You know, somebody taught me long ago the "principle of the four drawers". Maybe it will help you to deepen and improve the identification of the causes and factors of the problems. The drawers are:

Equipment	Material	Method	Person

I noticed that most of your questions were focused on people without referring to the other three drawers." Then, he added mischievously, that it was not even a problem of material, such as perfume, that angered Shulamit, because of the fact that she became relaxed the moment that Steve moved away... But, my dear Steve, I do suggest you try to explore and find out the process, the method, and the backlog of factors whose activity in a particular order creates mutual influences.

The mechanic became serious again and said, "You know,

each engine moves to a higher column by providing it with a richer mix of fuel and air. Let's look for the process that causes Rebecca to increase aggression."

Steve looked at him, surprised and thoughtful, and said, "It seems to me that I will give up my psychologist and ask you to analyze my wife and her relationship with the environment." The mechanic burst out laughing and declared that, "You can use "common sense" at all areas of life.

Steve concluded seriously, "Okay, I realize that I tried to give answers to each of the five indexes, but I forgot that every parameter has four drawers and I related only to the drawer of people. Yes, you are right said the mechanic. In the past I was in your position and I decided to build an ordered and friendly system which is called "The twenty drawer table" that allows me to get the full picture, and the reciprocal relations and influences between its components.

If it suits you, I'd love to give it to you, provided you promise you will practice using it for simple things before you go for complicated problems. It seems a bit boring initially, but it is worth trying and practicing because

The table will help and be very useful in places and situations where efforts that are based on intuition, experience, and experimentation get stuck!

With this table, dear Steve, you can perhaps even solve the puzzle of your wife, Shulamit." Now Steve was smiling and said it was worth a try, basically because he had never thought before to put his wife's behavior into drawers or a table.

The twenty drawer table

	Essence what	Timing when	Scope, size How many How much	location where	Trend Direction and development
Person	1	2	3	4	5
Material Of all kinds	6	7	8	9	10
Equip-ment means	11	12	13	14	15
Method how	16	17	18	19	20

The mechanic added that it was important not to skip any drawer and that there might be cases that after checking, he would come to the conclusion that there are drawers that remain empty, which means that there is no information to put into those drawers .

To show Steve how to work with the table, the mechanic demonstrated questions that were relevant to certain drawers.

2 - Timing/Person- When does the person first appear in the area of phenomenon?

   - At the time he was there, were there any other people?
   -What did the person do when, and if, the others left?

9 - Location/Material – Where was the part when the problem was created?

   - Where was the part when the problem was fixed?
   - Where was the part when it was reinstated?
   - Where is the part's defect?

11 - Equipment/Essence – Which tools or instruments were used?

7 - Material/Timing – Was any substance dispersed during aggression?

10 - Location/Method- How did the man fall into the bucket?

It is worth noting the use of the question indicators of **what, when, where, who, which, how.** These questions seek facts (Do you remember? We said that first we are looking through our "exist" glasses!). It is also worth paying attention to the face that there was no use of the word why—meaning no explanation or interpretation—describing relationships and mutual influences among facts that happened.

The order of questioning is not coincidental. It illustrates the rule:

Preference should be given to gathering information about the facts connected to the situation and the effort to identify the causes. The more facts you gather, so will your chance to increase the correct detection of the cause of the problem.

Ask fact-collecting questions first:
What, When, Where, how, did it happen?

It is preferred to ask why only after you've collected all of these; if you can find the explanation of the mutual influences between the facts and you are sure about them, it seems that you have made a full diagnosis of the problem..

Now it is the right time to recall the "Funnel law". We remember that it is necessary to isolate relevant and influential facts. It is possible that we may have collected in our drawers facts that do not affect the issue at hand. The practical and effective tested way to do it is by using **contrary questions**.

A few examples:

Timing/Person – If we had previously only asked: When he was there, were Catherine and Tom there, too? Now we will continue to ask: Do you know for sure that there were no other people?

Equipment/Essence – If we had previously only asked: Which tools or devices were used, Now, we will continue to ask: Do we know with certainty which instruments we did *not* use?

Now, if we go to Steve's problems, we can illustrate that by adding contrary questions, Steve can build confidence in the relevant information by asking:

	Previous information-hypothesis	Contrary questions
Essence	Shulamit behaves like this only to Rebecca.	Is it possible that Shulamit behaves like this to other people?
Location	It happens only when Steve is around.	Are you sure that it does not happen when Steve is not around?
Timing	It seems to Steve that it happened after Ingrid told Shulamit about the fights between Max and Rebecca. Steve also recalled that before marriage, when Shulamit was a friend of Howard's, she behaved similarly to Angelica who was beautiful and charming.	Could this have happed to Shulamit in other cases?
Scope and size	Aggression always appears at the beginning of the evening, after Steve feels uneasy and moves away from Max and Rebecca. Then his wife becomes more pleasant to Rebecca.	Is there any possibility that aggression will appear in other times during the evening? Is there a possibility that Shulamit continued being unpleasant to Rebecca and Steve but he simply did not see it?
Trend	To Steve, it seems that Shulamit's behavior became permanent	Are there situations of meeting with couples where Shulamit is not aggressive?

> The more I am confident about what happened and the more I can identify by using contrary questions what certainly did *not* happen, I gain my ability to identify the factors that created the problem.

For the sake of maintaining our ability to effectively use the logical rules of the advanced common sense, all we have to do is to remember the following chart that supplies a full picture on how to use the methodology.

SUMMARY OF THE DIAGNOSTIC PROCESS

Essence Location Timing Scope and size Trend

↓ ↓ ↓ ↓ ↓

After you know the standard normal and correct State, Ask question from a macro perspective to a micro point of view

↓

Ask contrary questions

↓ ↓ ↓

THIS IS THE TIME AND PLACE TO SPECULATE ABOUT THE CAUSES OF THE PHENOMENA

You have probably noticed that I have used the concept of "established hypothesis," that emphasizes the fact that I still do not have full confidence in identifying the causes of the phenomenon. Further verification process is needed in order for us to be certain about the factors (Or, alternatively, it turns out that we were wrong, and then we have to redo the entire process.)

Let's go back to Steve and Shulamit. For the sake of simplicity, let us assume that all the contrary\opposing questions that Steve asked led to the confirmation of his hypotheses and that no new facts were added.

We will focus on the following facts:

1. When Steve moves away from Rebecca, Shulamit is not aggressive toward her or toward Steve.
2. Shulamit did the same with Howard and Angelica when she was with her former partner.
3. Shulamit knows that Rebecca does not live in peace with her partner.

Our well-founded hypothesis would be that the trigger for Shulamit's aggression is always her partner's behavior. Every time Steve or Howard, Shulamit's partners, come over and talk to a lady with whom they have a close acquaintance, Shulamit becomes aggressive, and it does not matter when or where it happens.

Now it is time to consider the possible cause

> **When the possible cause exists, the malfunction is there. When the possible cause does not exist, the malfunction does not exist**

We have the additional information that when Steve moves away and does not speak to Rebecca, Shulamit calms down. We also know that Shulamit behaved similarly when she was with Howard. There is no choice but to conclude that when Shulamit's partner (no matter who he is) talks to a lady that is a close friend whom he has known for years, Shulamit becomes aggressive. We can stop here and suggest a very practical solution that tells Steve not to get close to past friends, especially women. In that case, we are sure that there will be no aggression from Shulamit. But…

A. we are not certain that Steve is willing to pay the price of the preventive behavior of disengagement and the need of acting so cautiously every time that Shulamit is close.
B. It is quite certain that Shulamit's next partner will suffer the same behavior if he will not be warned by Steve or… maybe Shulamit herself.

Common sense leads us to the conclusion that we have identified a factor that is a symptom of another more primary factor. Success in his identification will enable control and prevention of aggression by avoiding at least the creation of situations that are stimulating and thus increase

Shulamit's aggression.

Taking a step forward leads to the essential conclusion that we have to redefine the problem. A definition that invites us to examine why in these situations Shulamit becomes aggressive—no matter who is next to her!

With regard to the fact that we have already isolated and understood the components and the environment of the phenomenon, we should not go back and restart the whole process as most of us may think (unless there is a necessity that we might find out if the next step fails). What is required to do now, is to focus, deepen and analyze the new definition by the "why chain".

> **The "why chain" is an effective tool to fully explain the rationale, contexts and status of the identified factor or factors.**
>
> **The why chain is the explanation of the chain of influences and connections between facts that exist or happened in the past.**

Now we shall ask Shulamit:

Why 1 - Why do you get aggressive when Steve talks to Rebecca?
Because I know that Rebecca likes Steve very much!

Why 2 - Why do you become aggressive because Rebecca likes Steve?

Because men can be seduced very easily, and certainly one as successful as Steve. He never stops looking and staring, just like Howard !

Why 3 - Why do you fear that Steve will be tempted?
Are you kidding me? I know that both Rebecca and Angelica are much more attractive than I am.

Why 4 - Why do you think you are less attractive?
Tell me, do you really not see that I'm both a little fat and short, and they are tall and thin?

Why 5 - Why do you think that being fat and short is less attractive? Why do you think that Steve likes tall women? He chose you!
Because Steve treats and sees me as a given. He never tells me how much he loves me, and to my best friends, who look at him with an inviting look, he is always so nice and charming.

Why 6 - Why you do not ask him what he thinks or feels of you?
The truth is because I am afraid of the answer and I am more comfortable without it!

Why 7 - Why are you afraid of the answer? What can frighten you so badly?

That he will leave me like everyone does.

And here we stopped and asked Shulamit whether she was aware of the fact that out of fear that Steve would leave her, she acted aggressively every time Steve was close to friends who were important to him. Was she aware of the fact that by this behavior, she was creating tensions, embarrassment and dissatisfaction that really could eventually cause Steve to leave her?

Shulamit was silent for two long minutes and then said quietly, "I never thought of it that way. Thank you for your **advanced common sense** that made me realize and finally become aware that I am the one who creates the tensions and I am the one who should expect myself to change!

> **Clever and gradual use of the "why chain" led to a better and deepened diagnosis that helped to reach the initial factors that caused the phenomenon or malfunction .**

Usually we will not have to dig in through seven stages. There is most often a good chance that after three or four times of questioning, we will reach the causes of the problem.

Now that the cause is identified, Shulamit has to decide what to do with her insight, or in other words, **make a decision regarding what solution to choose and implement.**

The first option:
To meet Steve and expose and share her insight, making an effort to reduce the consequences created by her behavior.

To try to make Steve understand that her aggression is due to her fears and weaknesses. If she succeeds, it will make Steve more satisfied and calm, and eventually stop blaming himself and feeling guilty when he wasn't doing anything wrong.

The second option:
To not to be aggressive in situations similar to those that previously arose her aggression and to try to be nice and polite, even when the fears are almost overwhelming.

The third option:
To use both options and perhaps to ask Steve to give her a feedback by an agreed sign in real time, before she loses control. An alternative, which is much better than being polite with an artificial smile that keeps her blind and un-aware of the tension and frustrations that she creates in Steve again and again.

> **Please stop for a minute and ask yourself at this junction what would you do if you were Shulamit ?**

To help Shulamit at this juncture of decision making, we have to remember the dimension of Trend, that we expect to indicate whether:

- The phenomenon is weakening, growing or recurring?
- Linked to the past and ended in the past?
- Relates to the past but continues to influence the present?
- It may affect the future.

The **common sense** would prefer to be focused on preventing the emergence of aggression in similar situations later on in the future. **Common sense** would tell Shulamit to be aware of her behavior, keep control and avoid aggression.

Assuming Shulamit succeeds, then Steve is less likely to be harmed and there is a higher chance of improving their relationship.

This is the right time to add one more insight.

> **During the process of solving the problem and reaching the correct normal state, there are a number of action-options that we shall examine and test only after we are sure we have identified the factors that caused the problem.**

RISK ASSESSMENT OF THE IMPLEMENTATION OF SOLUTIONS

It is also important to check and try to prevent any risk that can appear during the implementation of the chosen option. Or in other words, it is important to ensure that we have all the way along Control of the processes, and all means that are active and used throughout the implementation of the solution.

Shulamit's main goal is to maintain proper relations with Steve. If Shulamit's effort to gain control over her behavior fails, she still has the additional option of sharing her anxieties with Steve and to try to build his understanding. By doing so, she will at least stop Steve from being embarrassed, frustrated or even blaming himself.

Let us stop the discussion for a minute and ask ourselves how many routes you know from home to work? What ensures your arrival on time? There is almost always an unexpected failure that carries the name " traffic jam".

Do you tend to choose only one solution, one way, that if you stick to it, you will merely wait it out? Yes, you can always decide to leave earlier. But you can also make a preparatory tour on a number of routes which are potential alternative solutions that you would be able to use when needed. I assume you will prefer a number of practical solutions with the ability to choose them on your way to the same purpose instead of being locked in a no-choice situation.

It is important to emphasize that:

> **Checking our ability and the risks of the implementation activities before actual practice, remains the last opportunity to improve planning and choose the preferred solution among the alternatives.**

Please pay attention to the fact that the more we invest in something, the more we feel obligated to it. (and vice versa, as grandmothers like to say, "Everything that comes easily also leaves easily". Once we have already started implementation, we accumulate more and more investments that will make it difficult for us to abandon or completely change the solution we have chosen.

Therefore, it is important to stop and examine it all carefully before we move from the **decision making** stage to the **actual implementation.** Be aware that the growing commitment to a chosen solution leads us in the case of difficulties to put much more time, effort, and money— beyond what we may have prepared for. The necessary conclusion is that we must make any needed effort to walk along the road with the most accurate process so that we can examine it thoroughly before starting.

It is also important to remember the characteristic phenomenon that many of us share. The time of deliberation during the process of decision making creates feelings of stress and uncertainty. The minute we start acting on those feelings, they become weakened or even reduced. Therefore, we can find ourselves again and again (and in many situations) with readiness to deepen errors and pay their price.

For example: while driving, you accidently entered a side road that you expect will lead you to the same destination as the main road. It took you a few miles before being aware enough to discover you'd made a mistake. That said, most of us will continue driving, knowing that it may be a longer drive on an uneven road, instead of deciding to turn around and return to the intersection and drive back to the preferred We can call it with a bit of humor " the law of the conservation of the route, keeping momentum through decision making" a law that is born from the very clear place of emotional preference of dealing with a semi-familiar situation instead of admitting you have made a mistake and there is a need to restart the decision! (Ego, my friends… ego).

Another example: most of us find ourselves disappointed after working in a workplace for several months because it fails to reach our expectations and dreams. But at the same time, most of us will hesitate to leave the place. Some of us are also busy to create for ourselves "explanations" as to why what is there is not so bad and maybe we can even find benefits from being there. The cause of our hesitation is a renewed feeling of uncertainty. Our fear of meeting fear once again.

The fear puts us in a state of uncertainty, although it may be that being in a confessional situation will be less threatening than we expected. Perhaps there will be a relative advantage because of our readiness to stop and stand in the junction of decision making and not waste our energy in being pressed to choose an immediate solution which avoids the option of acting with an open mind that examines different alternatives.

Therefore, it is preferred to adopt the approach that is represented by the expression that is referred to Napoleon, who told his dresser before a battle, "Dress me slowly because I am in a hurry." It is more beneficial to implement the principle that more planning of the applications enables us to increase the possibility of achieving the desired results along with keeping control of the process.

Let's go back to Shulamit for a moment and assume that she decided to choose the solution of sitting and talking to Steve. In this case, detailed planning of the "how" can increase the chance of success.

Planning the how means:

How would I invite him to the meeting?

When is he in a good mood? Will it increase the chance of his agreement?

Where is the most promising place you should talk, and will he feel comfortable enough to subsequently decrease the chances of him cutting the meeting short?

How much time it is valuable plan? Should we check that Steve or Shulamit have no other commitments that could prevent devoting more time than planned if it is needed?

How to avoid the influence of distracting factors or elements?

How should Shulamit dress?

In addition to the "how," Shulamit should think about defining the minimum purpose of the conversation. Perhaps it is difficult or not realistic to resolve all the residues and restore the relationship in one meeting.

For example, she can define to herself that the first two meetings are aiming only at creating a good view that will establish readiness for an open dialog from both sides as the process itself reduces tension and increases the chance of building mutual understanding. In fact, the minimal goal is the existence of the meetings.

The first consideration—the expected result

We need to define exactly what is the necessary solution, the *minimal solution* to which we must achieve because without it there is no move toward a positive situation. While choosing the necessary solution, we must prevent the effect of the fault—or at least most of it.

Let us meet again with Shulamit, who in her meeting with Steve, hadn't yet identified all the factors for her behavior. But they did agree that at the next party, Steve will give her an agreed upon signal whenever she starts a disgusting behavior. It does not solve everything, but it reduces the impact of Shulamit's behavior on Steve and her surroundings.

In most cases, we are in a situation where one problem or fault has several factors, each of them with a cumulative effect (direct or indirect) and a different intensity of the potential damage or benefit. Thus, it is important to:

1. Prepare all the list of identified causes and components of the problem.
2. To define for each factor the degree of influence and benefit that will be achieved when it is resolved.
3. To determine priority status in what will be addressed in order to achieve a maximal solution. (Unfortunately, we do not always have the capabilities and resources to handle everything).

It is important to remember that the more precisely we define the problem, the easier it will be to define the expected result. In partial exercise of common sense, we tend to "implement (in some cases without awareness) the intention of our solution within the definition of the problem. This is a trap that prevents free thinking of other possible solutions.

For example, my friend told me that he had a dilemma. He bought his wife a great new car and he had no other choice but to sell it and buy another one because his wife had strong back pain every time she was drove. The analysis of the causes brought to redefine the problem and led to the conclusion that a sufficient and satisfactory solution would be to replace the chair with an orthopedic one.

You will surely agree with me that it is a cheaper and simpler solution that will solve the problem with the ability to fit the chair to the needs, a solution that is not guaranteed in a purchase of a new car. My most probable assumption is that the process of binding the back pain with the need to replace the car was a result of past experience that had been reactivated on the present problem. This is a typical logical failure that assumes that past solutions are relevant and good for the present and maybe for the future as well—which is not necessarily true or valid.

The reliance on extensive experience creates excessive self-confidence that often leads to skipping above diagnostic stages during a semi-automatic state directly from symptom to incorrect solution extracted from the drawer. There is even a possibility that the source of pain is not necessarily only the chair and maybe that her back "contributes" more causes.

Another failure that appears in many of us, is the lack of distinction between a necessary solution and a desired one. When in an unfamiliar matter, the quick run to a desirable solution is sometimes the obstacle to deal with the real problem.

For example: My friend celebrated having a newborn son. Now they are a family of five, father, mother and three children. At the first meeting with Grandpa and Grandma who came to wish good luck, they requested help in moving to a larger apartment. They argued that it was difficult to raise three children when they couldn't each have their privacy. The cost of moving to a bigger apartment was estimated at about 150,000$.

Grandma immediately agreed that "there is no alternative", Grandpa looked on quietly. Then, in a bass, decisive voice, he announced slowly that he had no intention nor ability to "help them achieve that mad idea," especially when it meant it would take all of the grandparents' last savings. What's more, he added, was that they'd already helped "quite a bit" with buying them the three-room apartment they currently lived in.

After another thought, he quietly muttered in front of his frustrated family members, that it was possible to "make four out of three bedrooms. It was only a matter of moving walls".

The couple was "redirected" to a necessary solution! In retrospect, after examining all the influences of all the factors, the solution was found as a preferred one because the family remained in the same environment that they loved, the schools and kindergartens to which they were accustomed to, and with the friends and family they acquired in the neighborhood.

By the way, I forgot to mention... This solution cost a tenth of the estimated 150,000, culminating in no more than 15,000$.

We cannot force ourselves to push our desires aside, but common sense can lead to the desired solution, if only we examine potential influences and resources to their maximum.

The second consideration: the space of alternatives

After defining and understanding the actual situation and the required solution – the result – it is very important to map the maximum possibilities that depict the ways in which one might reach a solution. It is not necessary to play between the limited number of options that immediately come up. One of the best ways to do this is to "think outside of the box," to remove yourself from the standard conceptual framework that obviously leads to the same type and direction of solutions—meaning mostly solutions that are based on similar events in the past.

The recommended way to do this is to ask other questions! Questions that relate to the desired outcome of our diagnostic process. It is valuable to remember the statement attributed to Albert Einstein: "If you will ask the same questions, you will always get the same answers." Doing so is a proven recipe for failure. This is a closed loop of thought that does not lead to any new and different possibilities for a solution.

"He who was… is the one who will be."

For example: John's wife claims that she "never has enough money" and expects her husband to bring home at least 700$ more a month by working overtime. This is a typical pressure which in most cases does cause additional income but… doesn't solve the problem because it increases the willingness to spend the money.

More precise definitions, such as: "I want money available for the benefit of..." traveling abroad, for example, can, by using another set of questions that are aimed in a different focus (the focus of examining efficiency and reduction of expanses instead of searching for more income) ultimately create a saving fund solely for trips. Perhaps this is a more feasible way to achieve the desired outcome.

> **Remember! The success of increasing the number of alternatives is based on an expansive way of thinking that gathers more ideas and doesn't, at this stage, rule out options.**

Third consideration: cost

The concept of cost includes:

Money, time, equipment, materials, people, energy managerial focus. So too the alternatives we could have made with the same resources for other purposes.

Costs, saving, streamlining. They always contain a lot of ingredients. This can be likened to the reassembly of a bag of seeds that has fallen and dispersed. There will always be hidden cores, some of which we discover only in retrospect, if at all.

The significance of this reality is that when you estimate cost, you have to take into account those things that we forget to include, or were surprised and could not know about in advance. Put more academically, this is an analysis and risk management that always holds a measure of uncertainty.

The big fear is, as the common expression says, that "the monthly salary is fine, the problem is that the month is always too long." The money runs out before we reach the expected result. We still do not know whether there is stability and reliability in the solution, or that there is still a fear of a recurring malfunction that costs more money or time or energy. Therefore, we must always take a safety factor based on the best current knowledge related to the nature of the problem or problem being treated. In fact, it will be very difficult for us to make a cost estimate without giving ourselves an answer to a critical question about each of the items and actions of the solution.

The question is whether during the implementation of the solution to the problem, we are exposed to risks, delays, or additional costs. In the worst case, the probability of implementing the solution is less than the necessity of involving risk-enhancing and uncertain factors, on which we have no control and/or partial control.

For example: I took a taxi to the train station to go to the airport and fly on a business trip. After I left the taxi and got safely to the train station, I discovered to my surprise that there was a railway strike. At 02:00 AM, there were no taxis at the station, because all the passengers who wanted to get to the airport and arrived a few minutes before, already took every available car.

Of course, I did not make it on time. I left Israel on a

different flight a few hours later than the scheduled departure time. However, I still managed to do so with almost zero damage to my travel purposes. This is because I have a rule that every time I fly abroad for an important meeting, I take a one-day security interval, so, in spite of any surprises or delays, I still have a high chance of arriving on time.

For example: Never start fixing a dripping faucet when the plumbing shops are closed! There is a strange law in this universe, saying that you will always miss the unique rubber that you do not keep on hand.

You may be left without water at home because you have no choice but to close the main faucet and wait until the shops are opened.

Fourth consideration: the control subject: complexity, knowledge, means, materials. Processes.

Check if there are all needed means - and if they are under control in the right place and manner that is required. If there is a threat to the ability to control, please plan another way of problem solving. A solution that is based on the factors and components that you are sure you can control; a solution that considers the limitations and risks of uncontrolled elements.

It is important to note that the larger the scope, complexity and multiplicity of factors that influence the process of the solution, the more important it is to treat them more seriously and carefully.

In fact, we move without paying attention from an incorrect solution to a complex management process of fault management or events. If the management process is incorrect, it becomes a factor itself for failures and even risks, all in the process of implementing the solution.

The main elements we have to refer to include:

Means and equipment:

- Do they fit the nature of the problem and the problem?
- Are they in the right place? At the right time?
- Is the quantity sufficient for the task size?

Anyone who saw a fire truck with a ladder that reaches only eight floors, and comes to a building where there is an apartment fire on the twelfth floor, understands the meaning. Anyone who sees a single fire track fighting desperately with the growing flames before calling for help, realizes how much damage could be avoided.

Common sense will bring excess power off at the very beginning to increase the chance of fast treatment and avoidance of damage.

Did the fireman take into account:

Environment: (physical, business, political, social)
- Laws and regulations

- Environmental impacts and physical constraints
- Threats and risks

Those who have seen a bridge being swept away by the power of a river, only because the kinetic energy of the water stream wasn't taken into account when they decided to cut corners when the question of deepening the foundations arose, knows how harmful it happened to be.

Common sense treatment perhaps would have lifted the bridge beyond the statistics. Or deepened the foundations in advance. Or both.

Organization of activities and processes:

- Have you taken into account the nature of the relationship, the quality of coordination and collaboration among different professionals who are supposed to cooperate and work as a team in order to provide the solution?
- Was there someone who took the consideration and decision making aspects, and had the authority and responsibility of every action and role that took place in the process?
- Has anyone seen how the casting of a ceiling of a house is stopped by supervisors because the builders did not supply a sample of the concrete for the approval of the Standards Institute (regulations do not allow the continuation without approval).

- Anyone who was in a hospital emergency room where treatment was delayed due to backlog in the arrival of the results of tests, then found himself wondering who had designed the bottlenecks in the process?
- Anyone who experienced three workers who came to dig a narrow hole near the wall, even though there is enough space only for one worker to approach, surely understands the meaning.
- Anyone who finds himself going several times from house to car to load things for a walk, and eventually forgets a few items by the door of the home or vehicle, is experiencing a lack of organization of the activity.

Common sense would have made us understand that a critical part of the planning component of the activity is coordinating and synchronizing the activity, all while paying attention to the point of interface and overlapping of activities while avoiding bottlenecks—a skill that directors, producers or project managers should master.

People and their abilities:

- Is the level of willingness / motivation to help known?
- Is the skill, professionalism and knowledge required to perform present? *
- Are people available at the place and time needed?
- Anyone who saw a veteran mechanic who knew mechanics well, but was not up to date with equipment and computer checkers, saw a mechanic who was

probably and unconsciously switching the diagnostics to the mechanical side and avoiding electronic tests. The result is that it lengthens diagnostic time and increases the chances of error in the diagnosis or increases the chance of generating another malfunction while trying to locate the previous fault. Everybody will understand what is going on.

- Anyone who has experienced flying a specific expert to an event as a result of lack of local expertise, understands the meaning.

The meaning of teamwork:

When there is a need for a multi professional team, managerial ability is a must! Without it, the chance to create coordination, mutual support and functional activity that is not biased by personal interest or ego battles, is small. A cluster of many professional without the ability to manage them is a recipe for loss of control, greater risk, and in many cases, even create short or long-term damage.

- Those who have seen a surgery operating team know that when the doctor reaches his hand backwards, the required tool is provided and the anesthesiologist functions in a parallel process—done almost entirely without speaking. This is the meaning of effective coordination.
- Those who experienced a mall function wrong treatment in a complex process in a 24/7 plant in which the operator commissioned the mechanic to fix the problem

(and did not commission other relevant professionals at the same time as a team to solve the problem) will understand when later the mechanic claimed after checking that it is an electrical fault.. and the electrician that claimed that it is a software problem… it leads to a strong insight the meaning of mismatch and lack of synchronization that causes a few hours correction time instead of a much shorter period of time.

And, if we add the fact that between the arrival of one professional and the other it took hours, we will strongly understand that the lack of teamwork capabilities increases damages to equipment, materials and production time.

> **This is the time to emphasize that while you and your teammates are learning from this book, you are also building a common language and an agreed upon methodology to deal with faults and risks.**
>
> **The common sense methodology guarantees effective teamwork!**
>
> **It is common sense that helps everyone in any subject!**

Materials, quality, and availability:

When materials are needed, we must consider whether we have control over the availability, quality, and quantity that is required for repairs. In those cases, where the materials are pulled out of stock, your duty is to take care in your examination that no damage or defect occurred during shipping or storing.

- Anyone who experienced the sour smell when opening of a carton of milk, which is allegedly fresh, can easily deduce that the refrigeration in the distribution truck and / or the refrigerator in the store did not work.
- Anyone who had experienced cracks or dryness in the new tire wall he'd bought while being a careful customer who checked the manufacturing date, can assume that the tire had been stored close to the tin tire warehouse roof, experiencing a month or two of torture of staying in high heat...

The method: the process and the integration of activities toward successful consequences.

The lack of precise information about how to conduct an effective process can build a wrong process that will lead to poison instead of medicine or a bomb instead of light fireworks. Remember, there are irreversible processes! In order to achieve success by using the right process, you have to plan the correct timing, meaning, the interplay and definite influence between components and actions. The control of dosage and activities combinations (rate, intensity, direction, quantity), must be ensured.

- Those who have prepared and eaten stiff liver instead of a soft piece, understand that they had let the pan get too hot.
- Those who have drunk alcohol and gone out driving, confident and happy with their ability to drive, and his had suffered lightheadedness, understands, or at least is semi-aware of the fact that the influencing process of alcohol absorption has its own dynamics and time.

The practical common sense and wisdom guides us and dictates that if a particular process is done by you at the first time, make every effort to maximize your knowledge, command and control of each stage and activity.

I recently heard that a new driver was crushed to death by the fall of his car as he began to lift his vehicle with the jack. It turned out he did not put anything in order to protect himself in case the jack would slip. He thought nothing about risk control and prevention and paid for it with his life. It seems that those who taught him were focused only on training how to drive and pass the licensing test and not how to deal with faults and malfunctions related to traffic or the right operation and handlings of the car.

Common sense recommends that as you find yourself making more and more diagnoses, decisions and problem solving on a particular topic that you specialize in, you should spend time to learn from both failures and successes.

Failure analysis will teach you how to do things differently and avoid mistakes.

Analyzing your successes will teach you how to recreate the activity that brought success.

I'd be sad to meet the person who looks in the mirror and says to himself:

> **First time—Wrong, a Mistake . Second time—Stupidity.**
>
> **Third time—malpractice. Fourth time—Malice!**

The meaning is that he makes every possible effort not (!) to exercise and use common sense. Perhaps he is even doing every effort (not necessarily consciously) to fail himself.

Usually it happens when you insist on trying troubleshooting repeatedly with the same way and the same tools, all without doing any learning or intelligent changes in some of the diagnostic activities. ("If you always ask the same questions, you will always get the same answers.")

There is a story attributed to Thomas Alva Edison's assistant who argued with Thomas regarding the reason why he did not despair after the 4999th experiment to find the right material for the filament in the electric lamp? Thomas's answer was the legacy of all of us and also the reason why we have light bulbs!

Thomas responded by saying that he found 4999 different ways how not to do the right way. He learned from his mistakes, took the time to analyze and refocus his experiments, and as a result the 5000th experiment brought us light!

Remember! Common sense includes constant learning and refinement of ways of colleting, diagnosis, planning and solutions. The opposite of the English rhyme: Remembers everything and learns nothing!

Solution:

The last step before realizing a problem to a solution is the phase of examining the ability application and reaching agreement from the affected people, especially those who have to live with it.

For example: You feel that your romantic life has become a boring desolation. In the back of your mind, you remember that your husband was a very enthusiastic romantic when you slept outside in very dark nights without a moon and with millions of stars in the desert sky.

After calling his boss and arranging an anniversary holiday for him, and after explaining that you decided to make him a "planned surprise," and after sharing with him that you ordered a high-class hotel, all the while hiding the sleeping bags and the tent in the trunk… you happily announced that you will spend the night sleeping on the ground… "exactly as we did years ago" .

A few seconds later, you were shocked by his screams and protests as he drew your attention to the "fact" that he was no longer a kid and that only crazy people sleep on the earth! Even worse—how could she be so indifferent to his continual back pain?

Therefore:

> **During presenting the solution, it is important to focus attention in the expected results and their meaning for each of the influenced or involved people, and obtain the fullest possible agreements.**

Common sense tells us that it is important to remember and understand that the same result may provide different interests and meanings to different affected people. The more interests that we satisfy, the more cooperation in realization we achieve.

I remember the case of the father that wanted to buy a new car for his daughter for college graduation. As they both entered the car gallery, the seller offered him a powerful car that reaches 80 miles speed in five seconds. "she will be always the first at the beginning of traffic, when the green light is switched on and a few cars leap away as fast they can".

The seller was astonished that at the same time he got a warm smile from the daughter and a piercing gloomy look from the father who pulled her out of there. A week later, the father sent him a picture of the car she bought, a car that looked like a safe. In addition, the father noted the tin thickness along with the huge number of airbags on each side.

Common sense tells us that the seller acted in a wrong way. The seller increased the anxieties of the father who wanted to buy a safe car for his beloved daughter. The mistake sent the father to competitors. To allege guilt, I would argue that he still did not read "common sense for the advanced". Too bad for him!

Common sense also argues that it is important to present a description and reason for the chosen solution. By doing so, and by sharing there is a chance to achieve acceptance or at least creating deep understanding and reducing in advance possible objections of the people that have to live with the consequences.
   We should explain:

- How the diagnosis was done.
- Why the chosen solution is preferred over the other alternatives that came up.
- That we took everything into account, including constrains.
- That every participator was objective, or at least introduced his interests.
- That we considered all that is needed to do to avoid unwanted risks during execution of the solution.

I learned this when I could not figure out why all the faults at a cheese making assembly line in a factory kept happening about an hour after the morning shift ends at about 15:30. All the faults were electric breakdowns and they appeared again and again almost weekly. How? Why?

The power failure was the "human solution:' for the maintenance electrician to get a "salary increase". He got it by working in the evening in addition to the morning shift as a malfunctioning repairer a reality that he took advantage of and created an electrical fault every few days, using a timer that disabled machine activity. This delinquent act of creating a malfunction, deliberately added to his salary an overtime payment of 150% X4 hours for each "mock repair," which lasted about 20 minutes each time!

He was a smart electrician who understood the production process and knew that he was creating only a minimal amount damage. He knew it was possible to do all the production quantities that ought to be done during the evening shift, despite the short break. He also knew that the operators were glad that immediately after the beginning of the shift there was an opportunity to drink coffee without being bound to the line. There was almost without a doubt a "win-win" situation for everybody, or at least for the operators and the maintenance personnel.

In presenting the "doing manner" to details, please remember the most important rule in safe driving (and also in other subjects in life): **"Do not cause surprises, let the others know in advance."** When everyone knows what is going to happen at each stage—who will do what, when and where—the fear of uncertainty is reduced and the confidence in the solution process grows.

To embrace and remember this principle, you should remember the anxiety sweat and frustration that you suffered while sitting with your eyes closed on the dentist's chair, trying to figure out the sounds of his different, frightening activities that were going on in your mouth. You missed even the stab of anesthesia—without being ready. I am convinced that you will prefer a doctor who explains in real time what he is doing, what is expected, when there is a chance for more pain, and how long the torture will last, no?

Summary of the selection and implementation

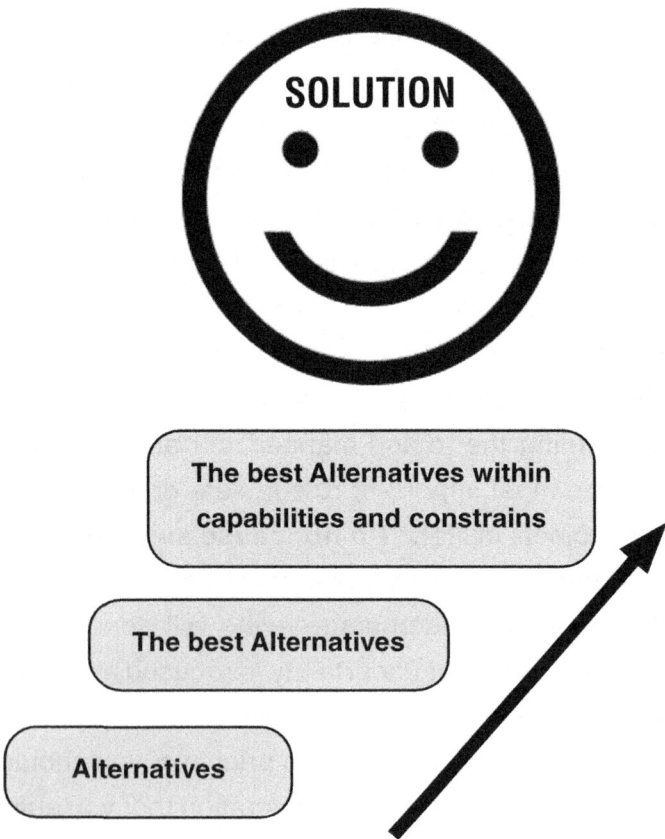

After learning how to deal with mishaps and incidents that were born in the past and are plaguing us in the present, let us try to learn

How to deal with future risks?

After all, there is a very high chance that I will have to repeatedly enter elevators, and perhaps even in the same building of the insurance company that I was stuck in. There is also a reasonable chance that Shulamit and Steve will continue to go out with their friends, all this while keeping the hope that Shulamit will be calm, without anxiety attacks. I guess that you will agree with me that when there is an identified chance or risk of a malfunction or recurrence that will appear without warning in the future, we should prepare for everything we can expect to happen. This assessment will, in most cases, enable to derive the benefits and prevent the potential damages from that event.

For example: My good friend rang me desperately and said that he hoped I had the telephone numbers of all the members of our university class. I most certainly did not. I asked him what had happened and why he was in such need of the list? I got an aggrieved reaction, seemingly out of context to my actual question.

He yelled that the phone technician that installed the new Sim device, erased all his contacts—without the ability to recover the information. I tried to ask why he had no backup, but that only made him yell louder that, "Why instead of helping you decide to preach and lecture? Don't you think that I am aware of the fact that I am an idiot?" and then he hung up.

In the sudden silence I thought that I was not the sharpest pencil in the pencil case. I had no common sense! I did not try to understand and analyze the problem. I gave a theoretical solution that had no added value. Not only did I offer no help, I created a new glitch: he was now angry and insulted because he believed I'd laughed at him.

It all happened while I was almost starting to write the chapter of **Risk and Failure Prediction**. It happened because, despite knowing my best friend for so many years and being aware that he is a slightly hysterical person, and that his first instinct for every pressure or fault he suffers from is to call me, I did not prepare myself nor tried to plan on how to deal with the situation. Instead, I responded with a gut reaction.

An act of common sense was supposed to provide me with a recipe for the next hysterical call that surely would come. I add a sin to the crime and addressed the information and equipment problem and not the person himself and his perception and feelings. It is indeed a misdiagnosis and a complete lack of solution planning.

A potential fall out of having had identified beforehand that I was, in actual fact, dealing with two different problems could have been:

1. My friends' hysterical pressure
2. Need for the phone number list.

Philosophically, if I want to make a serious root analysis that will build a long range solution, I have to ask another question: How can we lead my friend to be independent, have him stand on his own and not fall into pressure loops so easily?

156 | Dr. Tuvia Rinde, Phd.

PREDICTING RISKS, DEVIATIONS, AND FUTURE FAULTS

Each of us can find themselves in a prediction processes every time they raise their head from the ongoing activities and try to set their own plans and goals for the future.

Before entering the detailed discussion, it is important to remind you of the well-known distinction in the decision-making theories. **The distinction between a good decision and a right/correct decision.**

Right decision: The most reasonable decision that was made at the time of the event or the setting of a future goal. A decision that was made after considering all the effects and constrains on the one hand and the possible capabilities on the other, in order to realize what needed to be done.

A good decision: The decision that turned out to achieve the best result.

Of course, we will be happy when over time it becomes clear that our right decisions become good decisions. But, in practice, we encounter many situations in our daily lives that prove just that: **Not every good decision was correct at the time it was made, and not every right decision has proven to be a good one.**

This is due to a multitude of factors that require us to agree that we are not always capable to manage a sterile decision making process that exercises our common sense and integrity. It is because dimensions of uncertainty and lack of control do exist. That is worthwhile to understand and be ready to live with.

The first one, the built-in reality of forecasting processes:

Reality stemming from the fact that at the real time of decision making we most often lack: information, knowledge and insights on changes in trends, rhythmic, direction, intensity of movement, and the transfer of forces or new emerging factors.

The second, the subconscious, the influence of emotion and the instincts (which will be addressed later):

These effects are exacerbated by stress and uncertain situations or by temptation and opportunity to fulfill needs and desires on one hand o, the feeling of threat and rejection that we want to avoid or escape.

I would like to note that there are approaches and studies that claim that most of our behavior comes from the subconscious, without or with only a partial ability to control thinking or behaving by cognition. Extreme adoption of these approaches can negate any research and problem-solving methodology based on common sense and systematic thinking. On the contrary, there is ample evidence on a daily basis, of developing the ability to control and manage and conduct mind and cognition—a magnificent tool that manages itself.

For example: would you scream at your mother-in-law when she digs and grinds at you, ordering how to behave to her daughter and grandchildren—your wife and children—on the day she is expected to give money that will substantially help you move to a new apartment??

It is worth to remember and appreciate that, in summary, systematic research and logic brought into the world the most significant and major inventions, technologies, and knowledge, things that increase our capabilities on a daily basis, and which probably would not have existed otherwise.

The obvious conclusion and acknowledgement is that in order to maintain logical and mental functioning, we must make every possible effort on four issues:

1. **The essence** – A profound and accurate examination of the goals we really want to achieve.
2. **The process** – Investing in identifying potential deviation from the road map and realizing that we shall make all the way without skipping or negligence in dealing with the intermediate steps that lead to the goal.
3. **The repair** – Construction of active control systems that are capable of preventing and repairing possible deviations.
4. **Awareness of emotions** – Detaching and neutralizing its effects (to be expanded on later).

We usually enter a prediction stage when:

1. We are at a point in an **ongoing process** when we cannot refer and relate to the exact starting point because it is unknown.

For example: When was the first human created? Or, predicting the direction, course and speed of an approaching rain cloud. Or, your heart condition at 60 when you don't know your condition at 40 or 50.

2. In many cases, we also have no **metric or measurement, a standard** we can refer to and say we either succeeded or failed in planning and forecasting when we were eager for **a good decision.**

For example: learning bio-electronics today because it is the profession of the future? Or planting an apple orchard that will yield fruit in five years because we estimate that in that time, they will be profitable with a high price at the market.

3. In many of the processes and issues in which we make predictions, the end time—the end date, is unknown.

For example: the photovoltaic cell that we installed on the roof to produce electricity is expected to supply 100% of its capacity during the first five years and then, the supply energy will drop to 70% and in about ten years to 55%. From that time nobody knows if it will continue to function? Who really knows, after all, no one has experienced yet a full product life cycle.

Two essential conclusions are prerequisite for entering any forecasting process:

1. Invest the maximum possible effort in identifying and preparing tools and resources for dealing with all the phenomena and deviations you can predict. I always remember how much fun I had while having a safety pin or lanyard backpacks or collotype or patch or diarrhea meditation in my bag. It enabled me to continue traveling and functioning despite any unplanned surprises. They were also helpful when I was glad for not needing them. Knowing that they were with me gave me a sense of security in my adventures.

Common sense tells us that if you invest in careful planning and forecasting, you will be able to save your management attention and coping energy solely to the particular deviations that appear in real time, specifically those you could not expect. In other words, I suggest you invest in building the most effective way to be "lazy". Fluent activity with "positive boredom" stemming from once trying to regulate life to run in a semi-automatic and leisurely way. It means that your ability and energy will be kept for surprises and not spent inventing the wheel again and again.

2. **Do as much planning as you can. More so than you may deem necessary! assure yourself with high confidence margins, and dozens of counters more than planned.** Go beyond any mathematical or statistical calculation offers, even though they are based on all the information you have collected—something which will always be partial.

You can simulate the whole process to the preparatory process a traveler should go through while preparing a voyage in a new route. An experienced traveler with common sense acts with the leading basic assumption that the length and duration of the route and the amount of energy and resources that are needed should be multiplied by four or five times than the expected length and time. It is preferred to find yourself at the end of the journey with leftover of food, money and equipment than a lack during the journey that will prevent its realization or even finding yourself in a risky situation without ability to cope.

The typical failure is the absurd situation in which the more we need to plan and predict for a long term (which naturally causes greater uncertainty), the more we tend to rely on pseudo-logical calculations and statistics, and avoid using the very healthy coefficient of fear (not anxiety or panic) that gets us to over-estimating and planning.

A few examples for illustrating the principles:

Savings and pensions for the old age:
An old friend shared a smile when he spoke about a young and energetic insurance broker who offered him pension insurance forty years ego. The vigorous agent brought with him excel tables with future calculations of the cost of living, life expectancy, future life-style adjustment questionnaires and more. Tools that the insurance company had developed to improve the ability and confidence of the agent to make the **right decision** for the client—a decision that will prove itself in the future as **a good decision.** When I asked him for the meaning of the smile, he only laughed. He said that at that time, the capital amount from which the pension payments were derived was equivalent to the price of a four-room apartment plus a decent monthly salary. Nowadays… you can perhaps rent half a room. Feeling a little confused, I asked him what he had been living on. He smiled again and said, "I owe my living to my father. I was not smart or brilliant; my dad who was a "positive and constructive paranoid," bought with any spare money that he had, sandy lands in the middle of nowhere. Over the years, I built two condos. Some of them supply a monthly rental income and the others were sold."

It can be concluded that the principle of **over planning** made a decision that may not have been right, into an excellent and great decision. On the other hand, the logical and statistical planning led to bad consequences.

A typical glitch happened: life did not go according to the most intelligent Excel risk tables.

Designing SUVs:

An SUV enthusiast decided to fulfill a dream and build himself an ultimate vehicle. The process took many years of trial and error. Years during which the suspensions collapsed during a high-speed jump landing, the hard springs moved the surface blows to the spine, the height of the body above the ground and the engine power were always less than it was really needed. Some models were fantastic on the road but gave poor performances on terrain landscapes. Others had incredible terrain behavior for rock climbing or mud travel. But… if you cared for the driver's health, you had to bring them out on a haul. Today, the man fulfilled his dream with a highly successful vehicle, both on road and off road. Car engineers from all the companies come to his rural garage to see and learn. Most of them are highly impressed by the wonder, and the same question arises again and again. **"What did you do that we didn't?"**

The direct and honest answer was a little insulting and yet thought provoking. **" I simply applied common sense— common sense that to others seemed to be crooked or wrong. Believe me, you are excellent engineers. I always used your maximum risk calculation as a minimum for mine and then multiplied by three or four times to be sure that I could count on all the components.** You are fine, it's only that my ability as an off-road expert to estimate and almost feel all dynamic pressures and loads exerted on the vehicle by the delusional, unexpected, not disciplined and unskilled driver operating in a cruel area and under pressure to perform his task is much higher than yours.

In fact, I added more safety factors to the previous multiplied calculations. I did it while considering the fact that I knew I could not predict, including all the expected and unexpected pressures and efforts.

Arguments that came up about high costs that would result a demand for a high price, created another smile because the guy decided from the first stages to use available and standard truck assemblies. During a two-year trial, it was also found that the maintenance's costs and number of breakdowns were negligible.

> **Remember: Increasing the success of forecasting and planning is a result of investing the maximum effort to predict all possible situations and to then make over-planning, which means preparing more than enough resources for the unexpected.**

Prediction principles:

In forecasting, we will continue to use the same tools for collection, analysis, selection and implementation that we have used but, the focus will be **toward future**.

The leading questions are focused on:

1. What can happen?
2. What level of control and assurance we have that the planning will be implemented as intended?
3. What are the chances and risks of deviation and changes that will fully or partially avoid the realization of the expected results?

For example: when we discuss future design elements that include materials, equipment, methods, processes, people, or infrastructure, we have to ask ourselves two questions during two stages:

A. The time interval between planning and realization.
B. During functioning after realization.

1. Is there information about expected changes like amplification, weakening, cyclicality, rate, extent, or power?
2. Can we build tools for controlling and preventing the effects of changes?

Illustrative examples:
- Fuel storage for future use. Whether in due course its features will remain? Will a corroding of the storage facility cause leakage before use?
- Airbag function during collision events. Over the years, is it possible for the sensitivity and the starting point of the sensors to change toward increasing / weakening sensitivity?
- Predicting the effect of a freezing malfunction when

leaving home for several days. Thus resulting in a possible increase in the temperature of the freezer and spoilage of the meat we put there.

- **The record of success, which is also the record of failure**. Jacob introduced to a group of about twenty business owners a new machine for making coffee, and supplied free coffee during their meeting. They tasted and enjoyed the coffee—cup after cup, heaping praise for the machine. At the end of the meeting, Jacob asked them if they are interested in ordering a coffee machine. Most of them raised their hands and ran to buy it right away! Jacob grabbed his head with his hands and mumbled, embarrassed, since he only had three machines and the supply of additional machines would only arrive in three months. Guess how many bought it? **ZERO!** They concluded that Jacob was not serious or a trustworthy seller. How could they trust the supply of the capsules? Poor Jacob. He has no chance of selling anything to them at least not for about seven years!

Common sense tells us that one of the most important tools we should use is periodic and consistent monitoring. This is why we use the tools and measures we have prepared in advance to preserve the design elements. In other words, we will identify specific aberrations and act in favor of:

1. **At a minimum**: identify the risks of deviations. Assuming that deviations cannot be treated, the focus remains on

creating tools for preventing or reducing expected damage.

For example:
- Prepare pooling containers near gasoline tanks. So, even if the tank leaks, the fuel will concentrate in the container and will not spread on the ground.
- Reserve a spare chute when parachuting. So, if the main chute is not opened, it is possible to open the extra parachute.

2. In the medium, partial control is returned, and so freezing and / or reducing the rate of deviations.

For example: blasting a flame retardant on a burning home so the fire rate slows down; the damage diminishes, and there is more left to save.

At the optimum: return the deflections to normal. That is only possible in a situation when we have a good prediction of the possibility of deviation from the correct state, and prepare a backup system to restore the functional abilities the system had upon activation.

For example: the ABS system is built to prevent wheel lock and loss of steering. Or, alternatively, the navigation system in the navigation software that recalculates and alerts when you have deviated from the planned route, returning you to the right path.

The practical and day-to-day significance of applying control to identify deviations in personal and working life is expressed in adopting habits, which are called in industrial language, Fracture maintenance, Planned maintenance and Preventative maintenance. They are all born to prevent malfunctions and / or the cost and damage of malfunctions.

Definitions of the different approaches:

- **Fracture maintenance**. Repair and return to function after the failure occurs.

For example: Replacing the laptop battery only after it has completely crashed.

Of course, it happens in the middle of a presentation you presented to hundreds of people...Too bad you didn't check the battery status from time to time. Were you under the impression it would last forever?

For example: Replacing the mattress only after springs are broken and your back suffers the consequences. Did you know that the typical mattress-life standard is 1000 hours of use?

- **Scheduled maintenance**. Have periodic testing to diagnose developing deviations, and at the time that a needed, corrective action is needed, take it.

For example: checking the depth of the tire slots in a

vehicle every six months or before winter, to see if they need replacement.

For example: periodic testing of all system detectors and cameras of the security system of your home or business, checking whether there is a need to correct damaged assemblies.

- **Preventive Maintenance**. existence of scheduled, corrective actions that prevent developing deviations from the normal state.

For example: Replace the water filter at the entrance of your apartment pipe every six months to prevent buildup of bacteria and contaminants.
For example: maintaining a diet and avoiding obesity so as not to have a heart attack.
For example: saving, "save your coins for a rainy day"- avoiding money shortages.

The decision on how to approach each matter comes from having predictions (if any) regarding the degree of control over the nature and magnitude of damage expected from event controls.
As the chance of control is small and the chance of damage increases, it is desirable that you avoid fracture maintenance and focus on prevention—or at least planned control!
Example: Do you check that you have enough money

and payment methods in your wallet before leaving home (planned maintenance) or do you find yourself apologizing to your friend and asking to borrow money from him because, to your surprise, you found out you were without money as soon as you wanted to pay for the meal (Fracture Maintenance)? Or perhaps you keep a separate compartment in your wallet, leaving a significantly higher amount of money there to prevent uncomfortable situations (preventive maintenance).

I assume that you will agree that common sense says that if: you are traveling abroad to a foreign place with no friends, maybe even without credit cards, you should take a predictive approach through prevention—even in case you may have been robbed. **Risk that is out of control but can be predictable** and handled by steps like

Taking with you more money than you expect to need or split it and store it in several places on your body and your bags to be sure you can continue to manage on your own is a good starting point.

Some insights we should all embrace: Waiting for malfunction.

We can afford the pleasure of letting things happen and break down only in those instances that we know for sure that the damage is small and the ability to restore a system to normal is immediate and in control. (Fracture maintenance with immediate retrievability / restoration capability)

Example: If the pencil tip is broken and I am in my home and have a knife nearby, my ability to re-sharpen it is instant and the repair and incident damage is zero.

Example: I forgot the clothes in the washing machine for a few hours after the washing ended and the clothes stink as a result! The cost of repairing the damage of the event is small, I can wash again, and it costs me a bit of electricity, water, and washing powder.

Controls:

Proper operation of controls depends on how much knowledge we have of active deviations. If we control and apply additional controls after the divergence is created, we are likely to encounter a phenomenon which we cannot cope with or rectify. In this case, instead of remediation, we find ourselves in restoration or renovation or rebuilding. Effort that requires many resources without knowing whether there are chances of success.

For example: The common man who "will make every effort," but will not go for a test of periodic effort and heart endurance. However, after the first bypass in the arteries, he will be most attentive with taking daily walks. "Fracture Maintenance." And not always with retrievability.

On the other hand, if he did those "scheduled maintenance" appointments—Periodic control—which, if necessary, would have involved intervention and treatment for repair with a most probable chance that only catheterization would be needed. He could have saved himself a lot of pain and health problems.

For example: The bachelor who hates wasting time baking and cleaning and tries to do some actions simultaneously, may find himself trying to rehabilitate the pot that had burned after the water evaporated when he tried to cook spaghetti…and at the same time, while attempting to collect the water from the floor, water that had run out of the bucket he wanted to fill, he also found out that he had to buy himself new trousers since he scorched the trouser leg with an iron.

Incorporating knowledge of **trends, pace, intensity, and cyclical deviation development** recognizes that planned maintenance is important for all types of subjects: work, family, company, property, etc., as well as the functional and technological aspects of the business life.

• It is important to deduce from the recent example that the lack of control (and of the control itself) over a process, in this case, self-behavior, produces in many cases a series of **"Chain mishaps"** that lead us to be shocked, surprised and frustrated, asking ourselves how we'd brought ourselves into this situation?

Common sense and the accumulated experience of learning in favor of future, offer the following rules.

FREQUENCY OF CONTROL DATES

Must be at least 10 times larger than the known frequency and periodicity of the phenomenon under study. Only then will we be able to catch deviations while allowing or at least reducing damage.

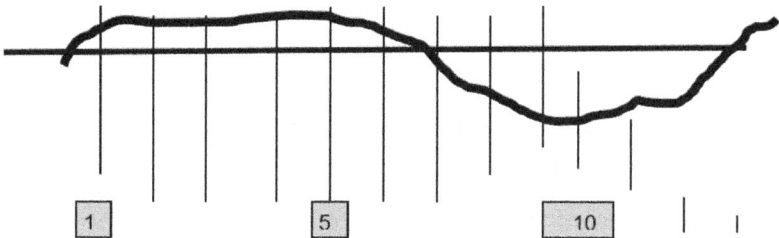

Examples: If the rate it takes to fill a bucket is ten minutes, check it every minute. Or, if the rate of evaporation of all the water from the macaroni pot is thirty minutes, check it every 3-5 minutes. Or, if an iron heats to a maximum in 3 minutes, do not leave the garment unattended for even twenty seconds.

Chances and Probabilities:
To allow ourselves to live in peace and without daily panic that our planning and predictions will fail, we must focus and put effort into all the tools we have **to try to set the probabilities for an eventual event and the extent and depth of the mishaps - and prepare coping tools.**

Example of "Fault Depth".

The probability of the collapse of the dam we built on the lake is only once every 50 years. It will happen when a rare state of continuous rain for more than a month accumulates in its drainage basin. I am not sure if I would be willing to live at the foot of the dam, because with its collapse, all the town and the area within the channel would be flooded. "Death is foreseeable." "The extent and depth of the disaster is expected. The amount and depth of the water. Its damage is expected to be enormous and not necessarily rehabilitative.

Example of the "Extent of the Fault"

The seamstress accidently simultaneously cut 30 fabrics for a size 38 sleeve instead of the size 42 needed for the shirt. She was wrong only once, but the result was 30 excessively short sleeves!

An example of "Depth and Extent of the Fault"

The juice concentrator factory manager wanted to be a very good supplier for the new customer and sent him 10,000 barrels of 101 liter concentrate instead of 100.

Seemingly, service goes beyond the expectations... In fact, though, the new customer returned the whole shipment with the barrels with that extra single liter since it was a deviation from the standard taste.

It is perfectly understandable why he was not ready to accept it. A team of several employees would have had to work manually for a few days to open every barrel and subtract one liter instead of the automated process of accurately pouring 100 liters into the water tank.

Back to the dam. Common sense says that along with dam planning and forecasting future possibilities of failure, we must solve two problems during **prediction and planning. The common sense tells us to act according to two guidelines:**

1

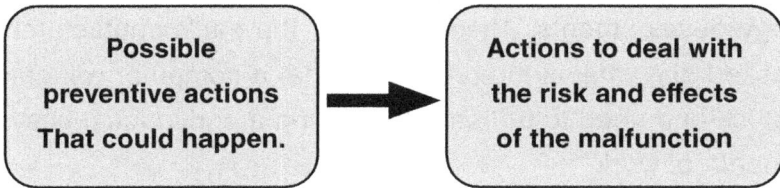

2

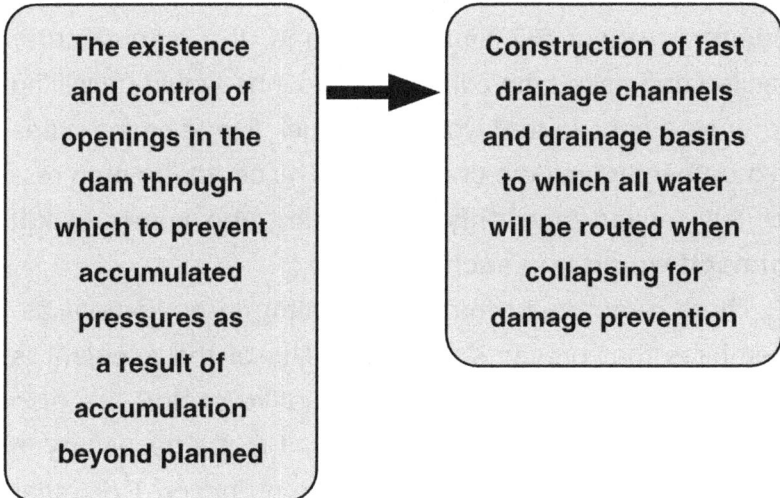

Placing both solutions and running them in the order described will greatly increase your chances of preventing the dam from collapsing. And even then, there is a process of channeling water, and reducing or preventing its possible damages.

A famous example of the chance and probability of malfunctions:
An arrogant computer man spoke to a car manufacturer and expressed his dissatisfaction with the pace of car technology developments. After reflection, the car manufacturer asked him what is the probability that a computer will get stuck and need to be restarted during a continuous, busy month of work.

The computer man answered that there was a chance that they would have to stop, shut down and restart the computer about 5-7 times. This time, the manufacturer smiled and asked the computer man if he would be willing to drive a vehicle that would get stuck five to seven times a month in the middle of the ride? The computer man resolutely replied that **"only a madman who wants to kill himself would buy such a vehicle."**

There is no doubt that the investing in equipment assemblies that prevents the possibility of the accident is a necessary decision in the automotive sector—it's also a desirable one. on the other hand, it is not necessary in the field of computing for information purposes. Computer malfunction will cause irritability and waste of time but not a critical damage.

Later in that conversation, the computer man expressed his opinion that the need to close and restart is "a characteristic of almost all types of computers... this made the man angry. "Imagine my telling you that "all the cars I produce come out with factory gate breakdowns and with a risk of stopping 5-7 times a month. See what responsibility I take, and to top that off, there's a warranty for recall that lasts years after a car exits the factory gate! That is if they ever want to go ahead and buy the cars I make.

Undoubtedly, in the computer industry, they rely very often on a symptomatic solution of taking action to deal with the risk by closing and restarting or, in a more complicated situation, debugging. The reason for this is the relatively small amount of damage to time and nerves.

* It is fair to point out that when it comes to command and control computers, the challenge of building a reliable computer is seen as necessary.

Let's summarize that:

> **It is necessary to have regular and continuous controls as a condition for creating prediction and prevention options.**

> **We must constantly consider everything: the components, the location, the timing, the process, and the standard that they work with - and so too the chance for change!**

You must set a **check list** of each control we must add in front of:

> **Action - The risk - The preventive or corrective action required**

Note: In the present age, when the complexity of assemblies, devices, technologies and processes increases, it is imperative to examine the programming and mutual effects between the components of the system. Those components had been shown **to produce chain effects in some cases, and reflect that under certain conditions, nothing happens, while under other conditions, they produce crises and faults. In the feasibility study, it is important, as far as possible, to bring to the table the maximum of options, including their bizarre ones.**

For example, the dog and the computer: Is it conceivable that the hairy Siberian house dog whose hair constantly falls out and who likes to cuddle under the desk at the owner's feet, burned the computer's power supply? At the first moment, the answer is no! But after a bit of information gathering, it was discovered that his fur blocked the computer's air intake vent, the air inlet was blocked, the heat increased, and the power supply unit did not get refrigerated and resulted in its burning! Yes, it makes sense, and it is simple. And it seems to me that most of us would not have realized the risks of having a dog sleep near the computer.

The Illusion of Prediction and Long-Term Planning:

The pace of change and technological advancement in the present era is increasing in a geometric column. This means that the level of uncertainty also increases with regard to long-term planning and forecasting. In some cases, we recognize that materials, technologies, methods, and processes vary to such an extent that it is necessary to perform **dynamic design, where we are led to two basic assumptions:**

1. There is no guarantee that we will come to the realization with the same components and assemblies we set off in the first place.
2. Increase the immediate contact and corrective feedback between the product and its users and the initial design stages to ensure more reliable forecasting. The best alternative is if you can have real-time feedback during the designing.

However, there is a high chance that you are going to be surprised!

Therefore, it is important to base future planning on flexible planning, where the underlying elements of decisions allow for a safe reach for resolution in various ways.

For the avoidance of doubt, this premise is complementary

and does not replace or contradict the prediction and prevention principles presented.

The carnival example: I decided to go to a carnival in Brazil after taking a trip in a rental car in South America. After two days, the car crashed. I was informed that it will take three days to get an alternate vehicle. It meant to missing the carnival opening and arriving late. So, I boarded a train that was stopped as a result of railroad hazards caused by a flood of water from heavy rains. The bus that came to pick us up was moaning and smoking up the mountain, so we abandoned it and took a taxi and finally reached the carnival. Who said there is only one way, or one kind of transportation vehicle get to a carnival?

Car's radio example: Whenever I bought a car, I installed the most up-to-date radio there was. First it was with tapes, the second was with discs, the third was with a USB socket, the fourth already had Bluetooth and Wi-Fi. For the fifth, I already talked on the phone through what was once called a radio and today considered a multimedia device.

If we put ourselves into the shoes of the device maker, we will realize that someone who had a fixed strategic plan on a particular technology (even if there was a huge organization dominating the market) risked himself.

Anyone who built a flexible system that could absorb and integrate new production and technology so quickly, could reinvent itself every time and stay in the market. The old people among us, please try to find a "Zenith" radio or a

"Bloupunkt" TV or a "Commodore" computer. None of them exist because they were not technologically renewed or reinvented.

Another example from Morse to thoughts: the cordless champions in the Morse key, were replaced by the teleprinter that was replaced by the fax, which was later replaced by the computer, which was replaced by the phone. And soon there will be a voice operation that makes typing unnecessary. Let's wait a little longer and we won't have to talk to convey thoughts either.

> **You can act like an ostrich and say this is the giant manufacturer's problem. But that's a mistake!**
>
> **It is the reality for all of us, a reality in which every wise person has to confront and reinvent himself. As a wise trader said, if the cucumbers do not sell, then I will sell tomatoes, and if that does not work out, then I will sell electric bicycles.**

EMOTION, INSTINCT, INTUITION AND THEIR INFLUENCE:

I believe everyone smiles to themselves in the driver's mirror when:

- They find themselves bending over as their car passes under a low bridge.
- They close their eyes as a barrage of water splashes on the windshield.
- They tilt their body against the slope as the vehicle tends to the side.
- They hold the door handle firmly in the dark.

Or, if they found themselves doing this during an ordinary daily activity:

- Recoiled in panic from an ant or a cockroach.
- Screaming while standing on the table because they saw a mouse.
- Bought a bag or a car or a dress that they didn't need

with the money they didn't have.

- Hurt his knees with long runs.
- Jumped from high rocks into a stream or spring... and closed his eyes with fear.

Surely you will agree with statements like:

- People or teams with common sense often tend not to run it.
- Many times, the fight or flight early reaction instinct dominates involuntary and even unconscious behavior (as individuals or groups).
- The actions due to emotion and instinct are much faster than actions of the mind. Shorter time between stimulus and response increases the chance of emotion and instinct victory.
- The effort of the mind to master emotion often ends in loss, even during continuous operations. "It took me a long time to realize that I was blind from love, frozen with fear, drunk with victory," and so on.

I guess most of us have encountered the feelings of:

- "I was uncomfortable with the seller, so I did not argue about the price."
- "I stood by the mixer like an idiot for fifteen minutes, hesitating whether or not to buy one in blue or in yellow. So, in the end I took gray ".

Emotions that lead us to escape from the ongoing deliberation into the warm lap of certainty, can be wrong. Emotions that reflect on being unreasonably anxious about situations of uncertainty to the extent that decisions are made too quickly, especially to shorten the deliberation phase. By the way, experienced sellers will know how to put you in the wits and redirect you to the next decision according to their interests.

**Uncertainty ⟶ hesitation ⟶ stress and haste
Activity ⟶ high chance of error**

There is a great deal of common sense in the ancient adage **"Hasten from the Devil,"** so it is worth trying to see if it is possible to increase control and use of common sense to reduce the effects of instinct and emotion that lead to immediate and erroneous actions.

Apply common sense; adopt the well-known rules:

- The wise will not enter a situation that a smart guy will (usually) get out of. Or, in other words, plan your life and behavior and try to avoid stress and uncertainty. This will reduce the chance of impulsive action and of making mistakes.
- If you are already under pressure or feel uncertainty, try to make time. Gaining time gives common sense the opportunity to make a contribution to your response planning, and so increase the likelihood of proper action.

I suppose that the response to these recommendations will be a skeptical smile with disbelief that these recommendations are nothing more than an ineffectual preaching, especially to those who have already acted on the basis of instinct and emotion.

Is that really the case? Maybe all the statements and examples above are wrong?

Perhaps common sense does also control stress and uncertainty? Maybe there are situations where common sense works in tandem with the emotion of instinct and even serves it? Maybe the instinctive behavior is too rational?

How would you relate to the following examples?
The story of the huge Mack truck and the small Fiat.

• While driving on the road, I saw an angry truck driver swearing, beeping his horn and "riding the tail end" of a fiat 500 Nancy that was driving slowly in front of him. Finally, the Fiat stopped completely. The driver of the truck descended furiously and ran aggressively toward the Fiat, cursing and waving his hands.

Then the fiat door slowly opened, and a huge tall muscular man came out of it. It took a tenth of a second until the truck driver who was a really a small dwarf stopped in his place, gave an apologetic smile, turned around and quickly ran back to the high cab where he felt safe.

We smile or laugh, and yet there is an interesting insight

to this story.

Common sense did a "status assessment" while running and changed the "instinct." The mind has mastered the instinct and turned the angry chase (fight) to a frightened retreat (**flight**) that was the right thing to do.

The Bear story:

It is a well-known story of two equipped travelers hiking up a mountain near a forest, and they suddenly discovered an angry grizzly bear that started chasing them. At first, they purposefully walked slowly so the bear would not understand that they were scared. The bear was not impressed and continued to reduce the distance between them quickly. They upped their speed… and so did the bear. They began to run, the bear quickly copying them.

The uphill was difficult to maneuver and the distance kept decreasing. Suddenly one of the hikers threw his backpack and accelerated his run. The other hiker shouted at him "Are you crazy, you lost your food and your sleeping bag!"

The hiker remained silent for a few seconds until he saw that the distance between him and his friend had increased, leaving the other closer to the bear. Just before being caught by the bear, the hiker closest to the bear heard his friend yell, "I will probably use your backpack—you will not need it anymore!"

Who said that in a frightened escape, you couldn't manage risks and that with a little bit of common sense, make sure that whoever caught by the bear would end up not being you!

For those of us who do not notice, I will draw attention to the fact that **common sense** in the design of odors causes the butterfly to fly in a zigzag that does not allow it to predict its course. The **practical wisdom** causes the deer to sharply break directions while experiencing a leopard on its tail and thus gain an advantageous distance. Because the tiger, in all his mass, continues straight for a few more meters until he stops and then accelerates again. Mice or rats do the same for cats. Soldiers also practice doing so in a fire zone.

The Art of common sense and love (the strongest emotion):

- Mary was in love with John but he "didn't pay her any attention". The tactic of trying to catch his gaze or smile did not help, and then she "happened" to be at the gate of the football field he used to play. (planned impulsivity that was made after rigorous intelligence work), holding, as if by chance, a science fiction booklet she knew he liked, then later asked to hear music she knew he liked too, all while wearing clothes she knew he'd notice. I know you're smiling by now.

Within a short time, John "decided" (or more correctly, was programmed to decide) that she was the girl of his dreams…. He wooed her with great vigor. Mary made his life "a little difficult," making it just hard enough for him to have a sense of achievement, after he fought for her attention, but not too hard so he would be desperate and give up). Love was in the air, Fervent romance and passion exists! Let us agree that Mary's common sense, which made all the effort to help her emotion, respectfully contributed to her success!

How does the mind's impact mechanism work, and how does it influence emotions?

In order for us to apply the conclusion to life in general and to stressful situations in particular, it is important to internalize the very basic and first explanation of how the main and relevant brain parts work. (The term brain refers and is mainly focused on the thinking, conscious, logical part.)

The first identification and analysis of reality comes from the instinct and emotion and possible energies that we consciously and subconsciously receive from the environment.

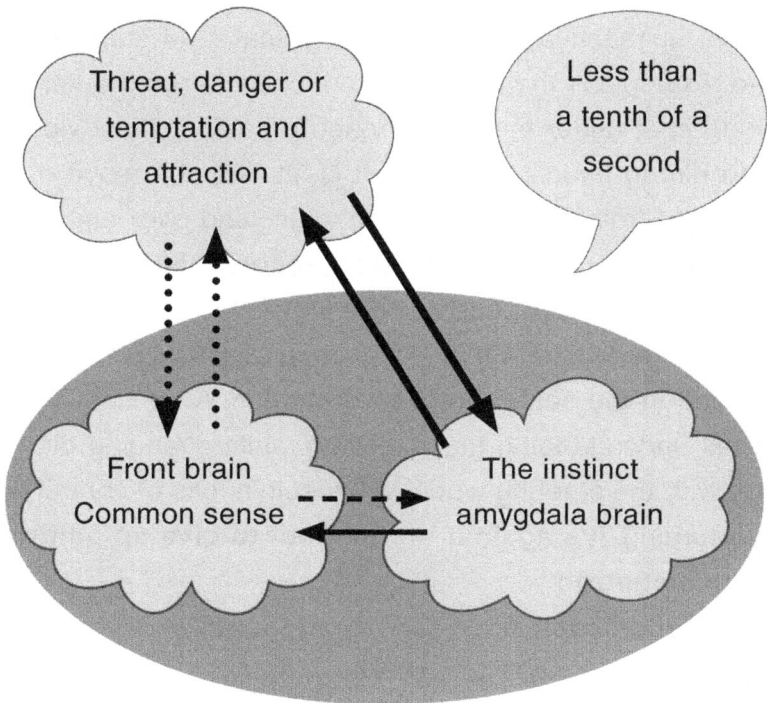

Fortunately, we have the ability to accustom ourselves to gaining increasing control of the anterior-front brain over the tonsil- amygdala brain. This ability is more developed in repetitive or predictable situations. Actions that are mostly repetitive with a predictable variation.

For example: Most of us can adapt and learn to drive a different vehicle than we are accustomed to shortly after learning to drive and acquire "semi-automatic" behaviors in a particular vehicle.

In some cases, absurd logic or values shape behaviors that go against the instinct, instead of the original instinctive active or reactive behavior. The typical, and sometimes sad, example is the soldier who decides to run the risk of being shot under fire even though a basic instinct would lead him to huddle and hide. It is, in fact, the result of a repeated training of controlling your mind over emotion. **Acquired behavior has become second nature instead of the original instinctive behavior.**

The experienced driver, for example, allows his vehicle to slide in the same direction of motion. A consequence of his understanding that breaking while changing direction with the steering wheel will result in loss of control or overturning. **It's against the instinct to give up control to gain control!**

You've probably been convinced that even in stressful situations **it is right to exercise common sense**, since you can always earn something. In the minimum case, you reduce the damage. In cases where surprises are rife, with completely new situations that you have not experienced and may not even have imagined, I highly suggest earning time to give the common sense the ability to work and influence using the four steps:

```
┌─────────────┐                    ┌─────────────┐
│  "stop"To   │                    │  Decision   │
│  estimate   │ ─────────────────▶ │  between    │
│  Situation  │                    │  Options    │
└─────────────┘                    └─────────────┘
                                          │
                                          ▼
┌─────────────┐                    ┌─────────────┐
│ Controlled  │                    │  Execution  │
│ execution   │ ◀───────────────── │  planning   │
└─────────────┘                    └─────────────┘
```

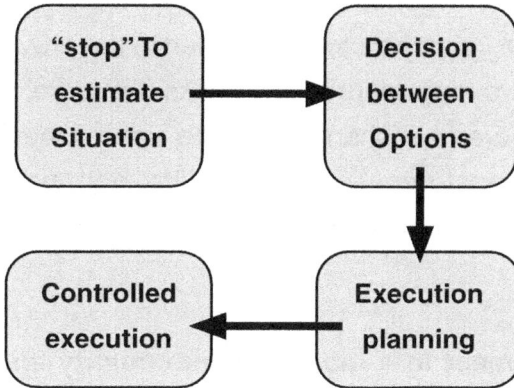

Every split second of time means increased mind control and "instinct response planning." The habit of taking a deep, relaxing breath for about two seconds, separating the stimulus from the response, makes all the difference.

The conclusion: It is important that we have the will and the sense that we are able to activate common sense and overcome instinctive reactions, even in stressful situations. In most cases this is possible.

To be easily convinced, we can remember that we learned to keep an open mouth at the dentist, even though we knew the treatment can be painful and the initial instinct is to shut our mouths or bite the dentist's hand.

We can also remember that we have learned to keep our eyes open when using eye drops.

In both cases, common sense has mastered the instinct, recognizing and appreciating that the long-term intrinsic benefit is preferred over immediate avoidance of unpleasantness or pain.

Let us agree that with a little consistency and persistence, we will use our common sense much more than before, using all the very basic tools provided in the previous chapters and avoiding failures and risks we were warned to identify. There is a chance that the use of the principles learned is most beneficial in daily life, both personal and professional. **The more we use it, the more we will enjoy it.**

When we meet in a more complex reality and we feel that there are:

Data ambiguity, lack of understanding of meaning, trends, location, interrelationships between topic elements, and **inability to turn information into meaningful knowledge and actionable conclusion,** it is advisable and helpful to try and use additional tools.

ASSIST TOOLBOX

Thinking and learning from our surroundings reveals that the use of tools is not merely a human race response. A monkey takes a cane to slurp honey. A beaver raises a dam to make it easier for him to fish. A spider prepares his net. A bird builds a nest. An ant builds a lament. Bees build a honeycomb. A mole builds escape hatches for itself. All these show that even when the mind is tiny, the decision to use it and also to use assistive tools exists! It is difficult to say whether these animals have innate or acquired insights, but examining each of the examples shows that there is a systematic, informed process and there are clear benefits.

I guess most of us are familiar with the saying **"Think before you act."** Those who act in this way, actually work in the three steps below. If they do it correctly, they gain increased chance of success and solution, risk reduction, time saving, etc.

1. Preliminary thinking and planning before action.
2. Thinking and correction during action.
3. Thinking and investing in repair after action, or agree

and be prepared to live with the unwanted results and continue functioning with the problem or malfunction.

The more we develop and improve the first stage—the preliminary thinking—the less we will pay in the next stages.

Examples: The carpenter who reads the assembly instructions in detail and guides himself to which side and angle the parts should be attached before completing the job. Or the dentist who prepares the drill set for himself before starting his torturing session, in order for him to keep the sequence and activity as short as possible. Or the architect who creates a sketch or computer simulation where homeowners can create and see their dreams come to life.

Or the mechanic who always keeps a pole with a magnet at the end for a quick and easy retraction of a bolt that drops from his hand into the engine gears. Or the washing machine technician who photographs all engine connections so that he can connect them correctly after the repair.

The common sense advice is to add to the opening position of "thinking before you act" also the consideration which says that it is permissible and desirable to seek the easier ways of coping, provided we are trained in how to use them. For this purpose, and once we have finished learning and implementing the basic tools that are common sense, we will help ourselves through the purchase of more thinking tools that will enable **advanced, systematic and convenient use of common sense.**

Controlling the thought process and operating phases of common sense are the permanent anchor that allows us to manage a situation with which we will solve any problem, glitch or prediction and prevent future risk. Knowledge and the ability to use the additional tools is made to further enhance the operation of the operating stages to deal with the complexity and greater complexity of fault and risk issues. It is important to understand that **we acquire the ability to lead a diagnostic and solution process, even in areas where we do not have all the knowledge and professional experience required.** The ability to manage the common sense methodology leads to an informed and systematic ability to lead and manage problem-solving, forecasting and risk-prevention processes while consulting with other people or databases that complement our deficiencies.

It is important to avoid typical and critical mistakes that very often are emotionally comfortable to delegate the responsibility to an advisor:

1. Responsibility for the solution.
2. Responsibility and willingness to lead the process and make use of the basics of common sense.

Adopt the principle: **it is possible and proper to delegate authority. It is impossible and wrong to delegate responsibility.** Controlling the logical process to its stages also allows you to manage the consultants and professionals who should help you.

The obvious conclusion for those who use common sense is whether you use one of the two options of:
1. Self-dealing with problems and incidents.
2. Teamwork and consulting with other people.

Reaching successful solutions that are effective is only possible when we lead skillfully and systematically (without skipping steps) in regard to the exercise of your common sense and that of your environment.

The practical implication is that even when we consult with others, **we continue to take responsibility for managing the solution process and control of the whole process.**

Let's go ahead and refine our capabilities by becoming familiar with other tools along with recommendations regarding what kind of tools to use for which kind of problem.

We progress from working with the basic common sense to the use of advanced common sense.

Self-test stop - I hope you did the few exercises that appeared in the book and even added and tried to analyze fault events or planning needs in your life.

If you have merely read this and not practiced, it is recommended!

> **Go back and read and practice again until you find yourself thinking and analyzing and looking at the world using the common sense "semi-automatically." You will find out that it will be much easier for you to learn and adopt the extra tools**

It is also suggested that you follow the guiding rule:

> **Acting with common sense and using pre-thinking tools will make it easier and improve the quality of implementation**

Take, for example, building a house.

During the thinking stage, some electrical currents and maybe some acids in the brain are activated.

During the planning computers and\or paper and pencil are also utilized.

During the execution there is cement, iron, sand, wood, workers and more.

At the error correction stage the uses of all the above resources are doubled.

I guess most of us would agree that as the stages progress, the amount of energy and materials and equipment used increases, as, of course, do the prices of the mistakes.

The tools I chose to suggest and explain their use are usually presented and recognized as standalone techniques. According to my information, they have never been presented and explained as part of a multi-pronged, clear-cut methodology and an illustration of the benefits of their combined use. Slow and meticulous reading and one or two attempts at gathering information or gaining insights through each of the tools presented, then later combining the use of the tools, will bring to effective use.

Next, in the concluding chapter of the book, you will receive the book's essence as the **7 Steps to acting effectively with your Common Sense practical wisdom.** At each stage, appropriate tools will also be offered to assist the successful implementation of the right solution.

It's a good idea to use the tools presented. They help a lot in:

- Targeting and defining the issue or decision topic for treatment.
- Prioritize different needs and decisions that appear simultaneously.
- Description of the subject in terms of: what, what is the scope, where, when, with whom, how, and why is happening?
- A comprehensive picture of all the components and factors that make up the topic.
- Identifying and analyzing the problem and\or topic factors while not getting stuck on the side effects.
- The most practical and simple informed solutions and decisions.
- Practical planning of the implementation of mental decisions.

Using the tools. Help without complicating.

If and when we have all the information, interactions, causes, constituents, and options available, we can keep the tools on hold.

However, there will always be a more complex reality that has more and more lasting effects, a reality in which the additional presented tools can help use your mind and also choose which tool is right and whether to use it.

The tools we add to the toolbox.

Below, each tool will be presented in detail and recommendations on the types of topics to solve or predict are recommended. (Alone or in combination with other tools).

1	Flowchart
2	Brainstorm
3	Chart causes result
4	Trend curve
5	Control curve
6	Pareto chart
7	Decision table
8	Gantt chart
9	Mind map
10	Processing chart

1. Flowchart

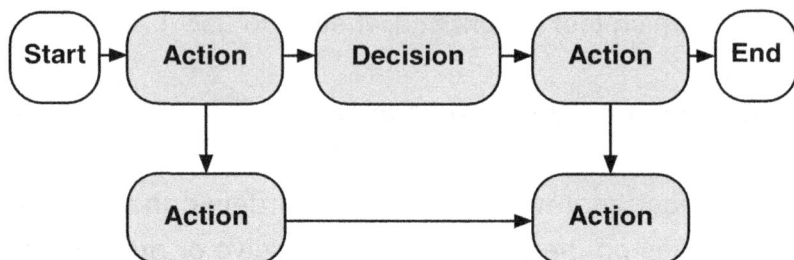

Usage:
- Arranged listings and description of steps and activities.
- Analyze and understand the steps in any process and be familiar with them.

It can be used for almost any multi-stage activity (and most of our lives are like this).

For example: cake preparation, getting dressed in the morning, home construction, writing steps.

Benefits:
- Mapping interactions and inter-stage operations.
- Identify vulnerabilities.
- Be sure that the sketched process is actually carried out.

Note: Professionals engaged in processes such as production engineers and system analysts have a set of graphic icons, with each icon representing a different type of activity (pickup, split, pause, decision, etc.)

Exercise 4 - Flowchart - Basic exercise for self-training.
One picture is worth a thousand words. Draw a flow chart of
the events below. Analyze your event chain as best you can.

What suggestion would you give Moshe for the prevention of similar events in the future?

- At 15:00, Moshe entered the manager's office and screamed at him that he could not stand the fact that he was searching for him all the time.
- At 11:00 to 11:20 there were short breaks in the power supply at Moshe's office.
- At 14:35, 14:40, and 14:46, the manager received phone calls from his wife who demanded that he come home urgently because she saw a mouse in the kitchen.
- At 14:00, Moshe received an angry phone call from the boss for submitting him an outdated report.
- At 13:00, the boss passed by Moshe's work post and stared blankly with unclear intent inside the room.
- At 12:30, Moshe went to the computer and found that he was disconnected and so he restarted it. He then sat down to concentrate on writing the report to the boss.
- At 11:10 the boss e-mailed Moshe with up-to-date data and requested that it appear in the report he was editing.
- At 14:30 the boss rang again and asked Moshe to come in at 15:00 with the report, even if not complete.
- When Moshe entered the boss's office at 15:00, the boss told him that he had reconsidered and came to the conclusion that the report could be finished tomorrow. He took his file awkwardly and quickly left the office.

He took his bag, smiled uncomfortably, and quickly left the office.
- At 15:15, an angry Moses returned to his office and began perusing the e-mails, where he also discovered an e-mail from the boss that was sent at 11:10.

Moshe burst into hysterical laughter and asked himself if he could slap the boss or maybe offer him psychiatric treatment?

What do you offer mosses and his manager in order to prevent or reduce the chance of events / malfunctions like this happening in the future?

Note: during the analysis it is useful to use a chronological flow chart of the events and also use the table of 20 frames.

2. Brainstorming.

A group meeting leads to better diagnosis and/or problem solving, sometimes including "out of the box" thinking. A meeting where the team can be made up of similar professionals and/or multidisciplinary staff.

The conditions for achieving success in brainstorming are:
- The consensus and understanding of all participants on the topic addressed.
- Equal weight of participants' opinions during the discussions.

- Existing rounds requiring expression and/or freedom of speech when it comes to ideas.
- A free-speech-discussion culture for the purpose of raising opinions and ideas.
- Absolute avoidance of criticism and evaluation of the ideas raised and/or about the participants.
- A lively and fast-paced process (ideas that do not come up in the first 15-20 minutes, would probably not appear during this round of brainstorming)

Usage:
Run a group of people to generate as many ideas as possible.

Note: When you are dealing with the problem alone, "make yourself into a few people" by examining the same problem at different times and while experiencing different moods, then finally choosing a solution from the alternative bank that you created.

Benefits:
- Creates lots of ideas in little time.
- Produces a supportive and open space that encourages people to express themselves freely and without inhibitions.

Exercise 5 - Brainstorming - Basic Exercise:
In celebrating 30 years of marriage, Steve and Shulamit, who we met in the previous chapters, want to indulge themselves in "something out of the ordinary." Their children,

204 | Dr. Tuvia Rinde, Phd.

Alon and Michal, want to pamper them, too. The dinner where they tried to think what would suit everyone ended with an "explosion" and general disagreement and they decided to call you, a wise neighbor, to help.

Please suggest a solution after reading their claims.

Shulamit thinks Steve would love to go out with his friends and have wine and listen to jazz. She loves jazz but is reluctant to spend time with her teammates and especially their nosy and tipsy wives.

Steve thinks that it is better to go alone—as a couple—for a vacation. He doesn't want his wife to get upset with his friends. He believes it is a better idea to rent a yacht for two days and have fun.

Alon, their son thinks that it is important to have a family gathering, a party perhaps, while taking a challenging hike, then end in Peta in the Jordan desert, somewhere he dearly wants to visit.

Michal, their daughter hoped for a solution that would require minimal energy. She suggested having a family dinner at the grandparents', being as it would be beautiful, respectable and cheap...and besides, it would save her preparing a meal!

Shulamit prefers to celebrate the anniversary with and without Steve. He will be having fun with the friends and she will be able to sit quietly and read a book.

Steve always prefers crowds and company, so retracting his previous idea, he prefers booking a great yacht cruise with a few friends. Only, he fears Shulamit's response and if she'll have angry outbursts again.

Michal thinks her parents are a little selfish, and in honor of their 30th anniversary celebration, the right decision would be to invite the children to a hotel for a few days of activity and shared entertainment.

All the family members are waiting for your urgent help before the family breaks apart by mutual "goodwill".

Note: It is recommended to scan the book back, and later examine the quality of the solution and the chances of it being accepted by all the family or at least most of them.

Note: In order to experiment more powerfully, you should take a number of people who will play the characters and represent their interests. It will be an interesting, experiential and abundant process for raising and exploring ideas that will come up as suggestions for resolution.

3.Cause result chart.

The chart is popularly known as the spine of the fish.

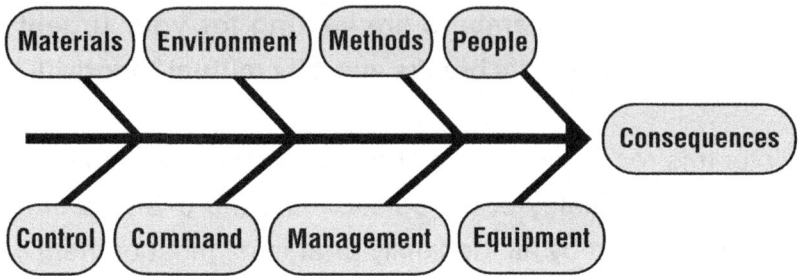

In complex situations, it is possible to refine and add detail to the chart by adding sub-branches

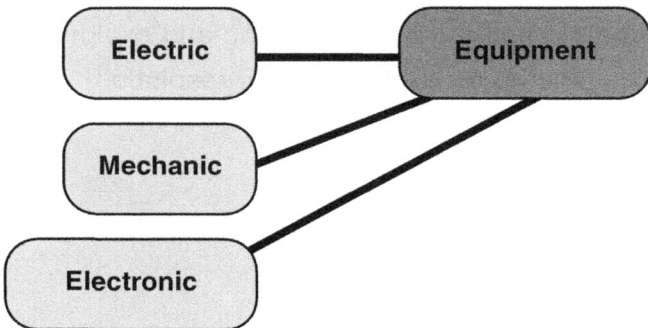

Work description:
1. Define the topic that needs resolving and write it down at the top of the fish.
2. Determine topics and key elements that can affect the outcome.
3. Try to list the factors by causal link (sometimes this is

impossible because several factors act and simultaneously influence both the outcome and each other)

4. Map in each category the reasons that contribute to the theme or problem.

5. When you have mapped out all the causes or reasons, you can also add a valued relative weight of the effect of the cause on the issue.

For example, you will map and define how to cut family spending components with the aim of reducing them to increase savings. Or, how will you map and define ways to reduce the impact of various components and factors on fuel consumption in your vehicle?

Usage:

- Allows you to map all possible reasons for having a topic or problem to solve.

Benefits:

Allows to distinguish between causes and side effects and outcomes.

> **In most cases, a topic, activity, situation or a single glitch has a lot of causes—and now you have a tool that helps to map them all.**

4. Trend curve

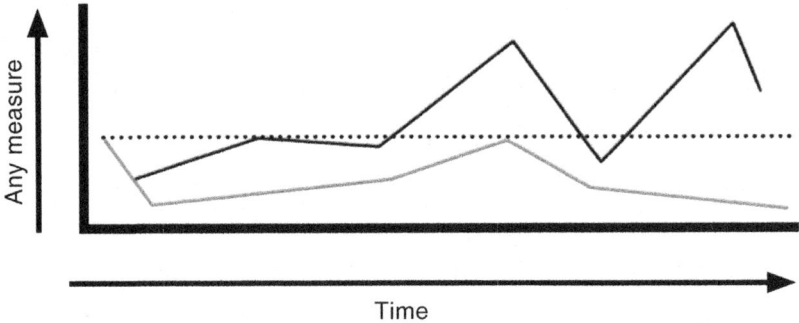

Usage:

- Examining how data changes over time. **For example:** blood pressure during a long run.
- Identify deviations with respect to another variable or average. **For example:** outdoor temperature throughout the year
- Examination of process stability. For example: The amount of butter the machine produces every hour.
- Comparison of variables. **For example**: Tire pressure versus outdoor temperature over time.

Benefits:

- Convenient and clear graphic presentation.
- Allows you to understand significant relationships in addition to raw numbers of data.

Enables you to predict the future, especially if mutual

influences or identified typical periodicity changes in be-havior of the subject.

Caution: We can identify trends if we remember not to fall into pseudo logical axioms like: "Any two points are con-nected only by one straight line." The axiom makes us forget most situations in reality, that between the two points the connection can be done by many other curved and broken lines.

5. Control curve:

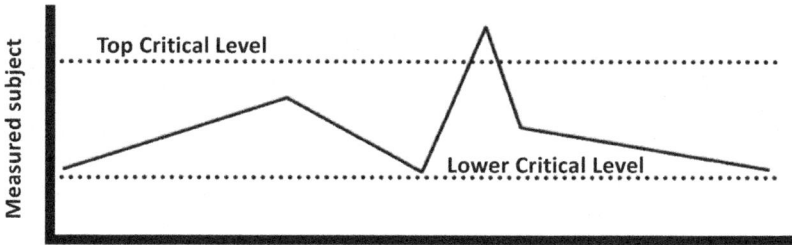

Usage:
- Checking the stability of a particular process over time. **For example**: Baby weight relative to age and others.
- Testing whether the process is under control or enter-ing risk and boundary conditions. **For example**: engine heat in the vehicle. Or red blood cell levels.
- Comparing current levels of behavior and system risk compared to past behavior. **For example**: air tempera-ture versus month of year, or seasonal income.

Benefits:

- A statistical tool that, if properly selected, provides sampling points. **More neutral facts and less subjective interpretation.**

- A tool to identify the influence of external factors on function and process, and afterwards also the ability to control and neutralize their impact. **For example**: A non-heating air conditioner that freezes on the outside when temperatures drop below 7 degrees Celsius. (Apparently, everything seems fine…it simply doesn't work) Or difficulties of breathing when it is not too hot and there is no alert regarding high humidity levels.

In the case of the air conditioner, the curve will provide us with information that the system is out of control and does not work, and it is advisable to use another heating device or install an anti-freezing component.

6. Pareto chart

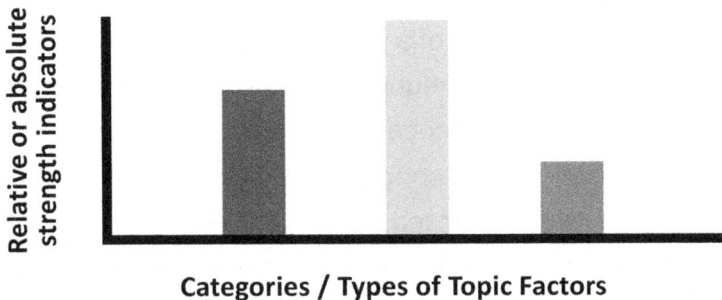

Relative or absolute strength indicators

Categories / Types of Topic Factors

Usage:

- The use of the chart mainly serves us to map problems or issues of multivariate factors or subjects.
- The basic assumption in the **"Pareto principle"** speaks to the fact that usually most of the effects of a certain phenomenon is due to a small number of factors. This principle is generally called **"The 80-20 principle".** It is most often expressed through the phrase "80% of the effects are caused by 20% of the causes.
- In the current application, the detail chart serves to describe a multitude of influencing factors on a particular phenomenon, all while pointing out the priority and / or relative severity of the impact of each factor. **For example**: Fuel savings is affected by tire condition, driving style, fuel quality, and the state of the road. The state of the injectors in the engine, amount of cargo, structure and shape of the vehicle, condition and quality of road and more factors, also contribute.

Using a Pareto chart will allow us to record the relative power of the impact and map if proper tires contribute to saving more than fuel quality and less than driving style and so on.

Benefits:

- Identify which of the factors are the most important influencers.
- Prioritize addressing phenomena or problems.
- Understanding that a 100% solution requires consideration of all factors and not only some.

As an example, try to map the factors of your time wasting or the family budget spending structure. In both cases, you will find that there is a significant gap between the subjective perception and the documentation of the objective data. **A detailed chart will prevent you from making the mistake of concentrating on solution efforts of topics that have only little influence, and will direct your focus to the main factors.**

Another common use that adds applied information is the comparison of charts of the same factors at different times or situations. This comparison allows one to get a complete picture of a subject, about its components and the relative strength of the components towards each other.

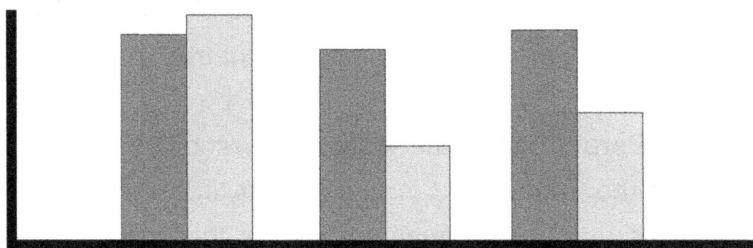

For example: Your electricity bill in the months October-November-December a year ago compared to the electricity bill for those months this year.

7. Decision table:

Topic	Car 1	Car 2	Car 3	Car 4
Color	6	9	10	9
Performance	8	6	10	5
Convenience	10	8	3	10
Negotiability	4	8	3	7
Price	5	7	6	8
Total	**33**	**38**	**32**	**39**

Usage:

- **Weighing and comparing some alternatives during decision making.** The first step is to define the features that make up the ideal solution while depending on usage, preferences, expected results, etc. This should be clear and decided upon before the various alternatives are exposed. Otherwise, there is the possibility that an important criterion has not been quantified and inserted into the table. The table will lead us to make a decision based only at the preferences we have built. **For example**: The person who found his dream car after many searches between all agencies; the perfect car that is best suited to his needs according to the decision table which he meticulously filled. Immediately after entering the car, he jumped out like a snake had bitten him and ran away. Why, you may ask? Because of the smell of the chair upholstery. That was not on the list of criteria that the buyer referred to. It never occurred to him that he was so sensitive to the smell.

- It is also possible to define the features which, if not otherwise specified, the decision taken would be not to buy, even if the other indicators were good. **For example**: Lack of marketability excludes buying, even if other criteria show positive outcomes.

- You can also define the relative weight and importance of a feature. **For example**: Performance = 40%. Price = 30%. Color = 1% and so on. If you added relative weight to each topic, then checked each attribute multiplied by its relative weight sum, the preferred solution is the one that receives the high amount.

Benefits:
- The table enables careful and measured decision making between alternatives. The table also reduces emotional input by separating predefined metrics from measurement when the potential buyer is exposed to alternatives.

- The table allows you to follow the decision-making process in stages, and if you want, you can recover and adjust decision metrics as needed.

- The table allows you to make a **group decision** in order by doing two steps:

1. Consents and commitment to criteria and their relative importance by defining the order of fulfillment of the assessments when testing the various alternatives.

2. Comparing the decisions of each member of the group and summarizing the consequences to an acceptable agreed upon by all.

8. Gantt chart.

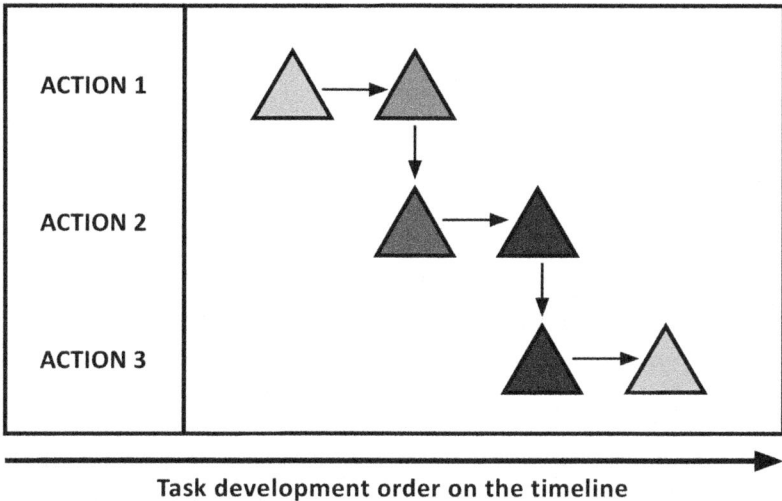

Task development order on the timeline

Usage:
- Planning a multi-task and activity schedule and monitoring the progress.
- The chart is used to graphically display tasks within multi-step activity; a shared timeline of starting from nano seconds through minutes, hours, days or even weeks and months. Like a pie-making project or building a car.
- The chart enables the synchronization of planning and monitoring of several activities in a chronological order.

- In the vertical axis, record the activity to be performed. In the horizontal axis, specify the duration of the activity of each action (the base of the triangle) and the time interval between action and action using the horizontal arrow length.
- In the vertical axis, we note the connections between the parts of the activity.

Benefits:
- Allows for planning and to schedule tasks, tracking them over time.
- Allows linking and tracking of multiple tasks in multiple domains simultaneously.
- Lists the main milestones or actions and their contexts.

For example: making sautéed vegetables:
A. Collecting and washing the vegetables. B. Cutting and mixing the vegetables. C. Grilling and greasing the vegetables. Heating the pan. E. Bouncing vegetables.

9. MIND MAP

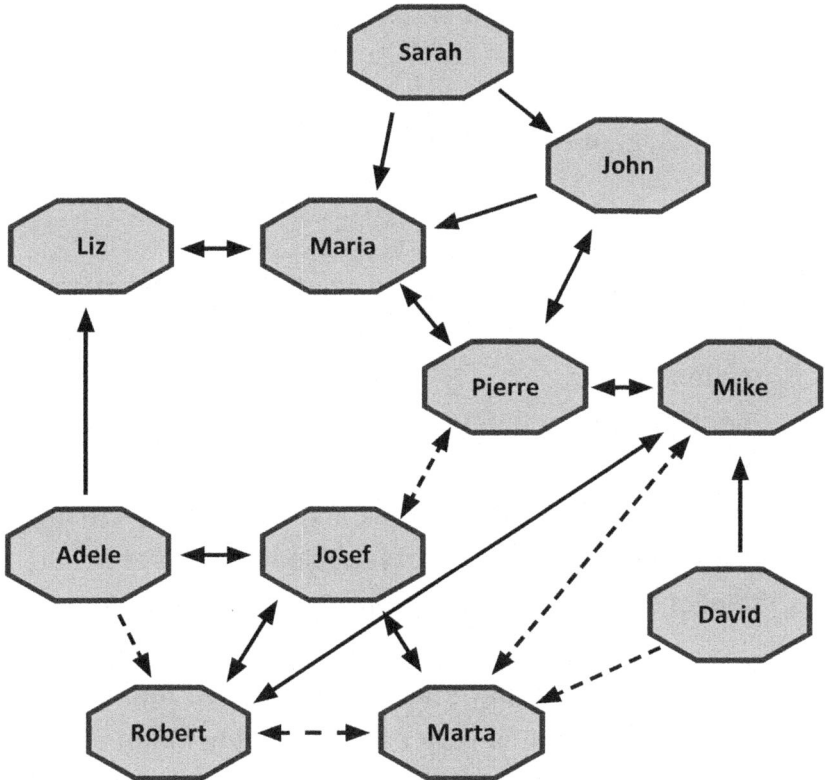

Usage:
- The mind map is mainly used to describe interactions between multiple points, components which have one or two-way effects between themselves.
- In the basic model described, an arrow type is used to indicate the intensity of the relationship (Continuous = strong, dashed = medium. Points = weak. Lack of arrow

= Lack of contact). An arrow is used to indicate who initiates and who receives the message.
- When we also want to describe the nature of the relationship, you can add character by the arrow connection.

HATE   **FRIENDS**
Liz ◄——— Maria ◄———► Marta

Benefits:
- A picture is worth a thousand words. You get an overall view of the nature of relationships, interactions and influences, etc.
- Identify who are the more dominant factors within the network.
- Ability to predict the potential impact of implementing a change in connections or participating factors on the relationship between the members of the system.

For example: Assuming that the map above represents social connections, it is very easy to identify Maria as an anchor and a social center that creates a close relationship, or to see that David is almost isolated and nobody addresses him.

**Of course, the mind map can be used
in any field.**

10. Map of activities at work.

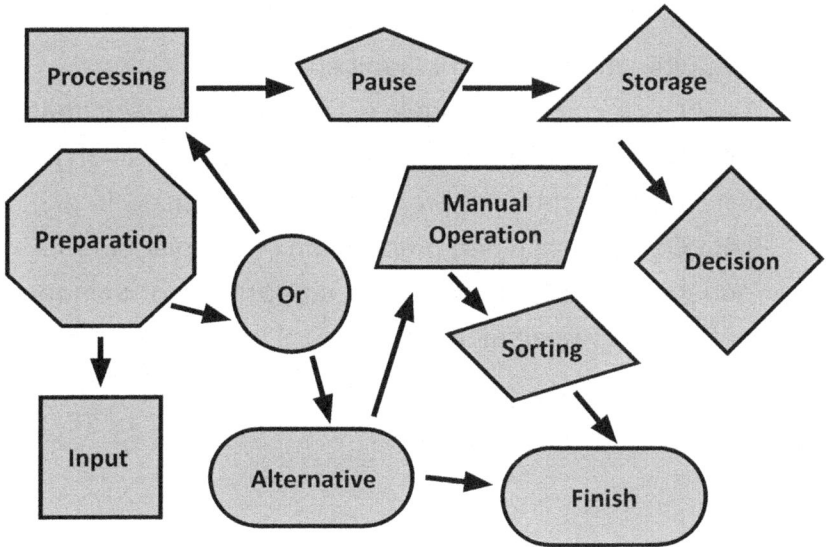

Usage:

- The work map comes from the world of symbols and concepts of operations, manufacturing engineering, organization and methods. **Note**: On a professional map, the caption inside or near the icon appears to indicate the type of operation when the icons that produce a multi-stage image of a process are not sufficient enough to accurately describe the activity.
- The map allows planning, control, command of various production or construction processes. It is often used as the basis for building operating and control panels in factories.

Benefits:

- Enables mapping a process that has a variety of activity types, describing the steps of the process as you go. (You can simply define the work map as a painting that gives the image of a few Gantt charts).

- It acts as a common language and symbol system that produces coordination between various professionals involved in a complex process. It can be used in any field. Complex cooking preparation, work planning for industrial or hotel kitchens, or preparation of cement making, chip designing, etc.

THE QUICK GUIDE TO COMMON SENSE. PRACTICAL WISDOM

Thank you for reading this carefully.

I hope you have also practiced solutions to your problems and glitches with all the previous chapters.

Are you wondering if you need to read an entire book to make a decision or solve one problem, or do you feel that I have created a difficulty that stops you from accessing your problem solving?

The answer is - surely not! There is a high chance that if you have studied and practiced the previous steps, you have brought yourself into a semi-automatic mode; **a mental state in which you can use Common sense for the advanced very quickly.** A situation where you can look at yourself from the outside and be conscious and in control while analyzing and planning your practical behavior. A Parallel thinking process that happens slightly before the actual behavior.

For example: the fact that while driving or dancing we are able to plan the following immediate actions while at the same time reading the environment map, talking to a friend, or listening to the radio.

The more deeply you know the process of using common sense and its phases, the faster the pace of intelligent solutions will arrive. We can find that the suggested steps can be done in a split second or within hours, depending on the goal set within the given situation.

For example:

There is a small tear or crack in your tire, presenting you with two options. You can either deduce that the malfunction occurred due to increasingly worn tires and that your best course of action is to order five new one (the spare included), replacing them all for a long term fix; or you can take a more immediate but temporary solution, choosing instead to fill the hole with foam and wait until the issue is, though just as important, also becomes urgent.

It is recommended that you use the:

**7-step method that is always correct
and always works!**

Planning the next steps

Objective

Stabilizing the solution

Thorough

Implementation and test results

Systematic

Examining and selecting solutions

A thorough understanding of the problem and its causes Allows an intelligent examination of solutions

Factor identification and analysis

Assessing an existing situation

Problem definition, the goal

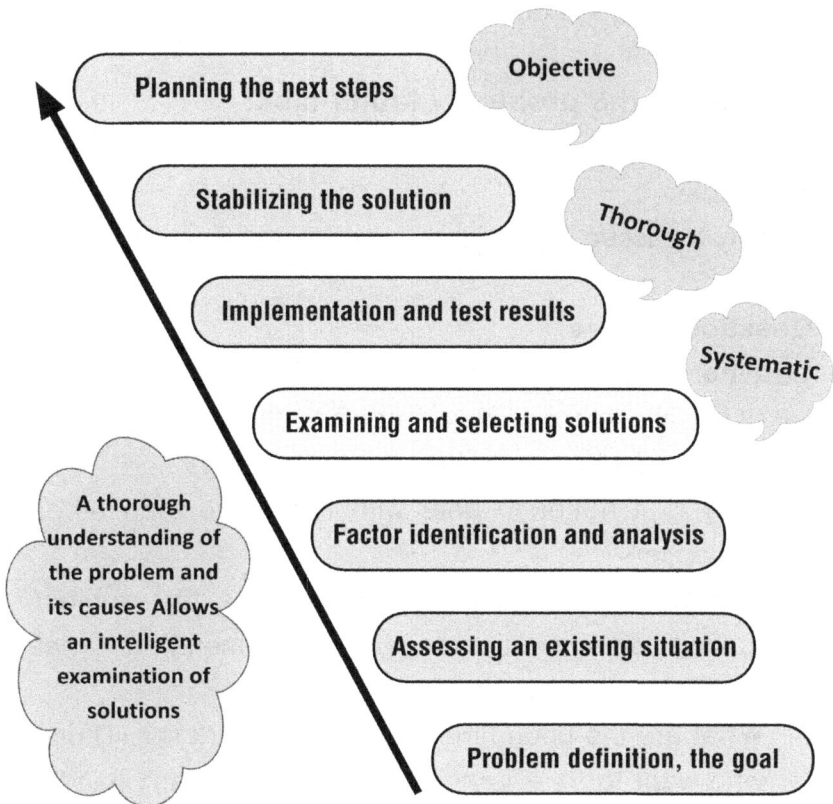

Use it both whether you intend to deepen and make **fundamental and slow decisions and solutions** processes, or in cases where there is a need for an **immediate solution to a problem**. Treat the method as navigation software that shows you the way! In this style, you will achieve the maximum possible benefits.

Each stage we will present the recommended tools to use.

These tools will serve us in cases where we want to deepen knowledge building and insights.

1. Defining the problem / fault / task:

Objective:
Identify the issue that requires care. State its importance.

Questions to use:
1. **What** is the gap between "existing," "needs," or "wants" (It is advisable to provide metrics for the need or want)?
2. **How** it affects or will affect the functioning?
3. **Why** is it better to deal with this issue than other influencers?
4. **Which** are the key elements related to the subject (people, equipment, materials, environment) and what are their needs or interests?
5. **What** are the boundaries we want to work in? (Those who want to fix everything in one stroke can't handle anything.)
6. **Is "first aid"** needed to prevent or reduce damage and impact before there is a solution?

If we managed the process correctly, we have, at this point, answers to:
1. The current undesirable situation.
2. Alternate mode—needed and desired.
3. Initial vision of treatment phases.

If the topic requires more complex identification of several factors and a more precise definition of the situation is needed, use the tools that help:

| 6. Pareto chart | 2. Brainstorming |

2. The current situation:

Objective:
Clarifying domain / boundaries / scope / intensity / problem trend / topic.

Questions to use:
1. In what way, steps, processes the problem was created and developed?
2. What are the criteria / parameters through which you can identify each stage of the process?
3. What data can be collected and analyzed?
4. What is the main focus?
5. Is any change in defining the problem required?
6. Is first aid needed to prevent damage / impact increase?

If we acted correctly at this stage, we now have **the Focus and Priorities on Treatment Issues.**

Tools we can use if there is a lot of data and need to build a wide image:

> 1. Flow Chart

> 4. Trend Curve

3. Factor identification and analysis:

Objective:
Identify and validate the underlying elements that make up the problem / situation / topic.

Caution: Many times we fail to see side effects / symptoms as causes.

Questions to use:
1. What possible underlying factors have been identified?
2. Are the basic factors ranked in order of priority and influence?
3. Is there a change in the definition of the solution needed?

If we acted correctly, we have:
A ranked list of identified and verified fundamental factors.

Tools used when there is a multiplicity of data and need for building and interacting and influencing:

2. Brainstorming	6. Pareto Chart
3. Causes/Result Chart	9. Mind Map

4. Solutions:

Objective:
1. Eliminating the basic causes of problem formation.
2. Building factors that help achieve a set goal.
3. Reducing or preventing the risk of recurrence.

Questions to use:
1. What are the possible alternatives for solving?
2. What are the constraints to consider when choosing the solution to implement?
3. To what extent will the actions we took cause the expected result?
4. What are the actions and what is the order of execution?
5. How will we monitor and measure progress step by step?

If we act correctly, we have at this stage:
1. Possible solutions and risks / prospects in their implementation.
2. A favorite and applicable solution?

3. Detailed activity / work / execution plan for implementation.

Tools to use when multiplying decision elements:

7. Decision Table   8. Gantt Chart   2. Brainstorming

5. Testing Results and Implications:

Objective:
Implementation of the solution design while examining its impact on the fundamental factors

Questions to use:
1. What is the current situation during the implementation of the solutions?
2. Is there proof that the solutions have eliminated the problem?
3. Are there any deviations from the intended purpose? Why?
4. Were new risks born that we did not anticipate?

If we worked correctly, we have at this stage:
Evidence that solutions make the planned impact on the problem factors.

Tools to use when multiplying decision elements:

| 4. Trend Curve | 5. Control Curve | 6. Pareto Chart |

6. Stabilization of the solution.

Objective:
Insert updates and changes to the solution process to ensure the solution is maintained over time.

Questions to use:
1. Are we aware of all the effects and processes that exist in the new solution?
2. What are the rules, habits, activities that will keep the solution for a long-term duration?
3. Which are the control mechanisms we regularly operate to maintain stability and prevent surprises?

If we act correctly, we have at this stage:
A logical and complete picture regarding the way everything fits and works while maintaining its proper conditions.

Tools to use when there are many decision elements.

| 10. Work map | 9. Mind map | 1.Flow chart |

7. Planning for the future:

Objective:
Estimating preliminary planning regarding where you go from where you are?

Questions to use:
1. What more issues do you need to solve?
2. What are the steps and plans to take?

If we act correctly, we have at this stage:
1. Results achieved versus planned results.
2. Knowledge and information that will help to analyze and handle events with similar content.
3. Improvement Process - A solution that may help to recover similar essence faults.

Tools to use when multiplying decision elements:

2. Brainstorming   3. Cause result chart

JUST BEFORE THE END

As I was about to finish this book, a large yellow bee landed on my arm.

I froze and didn't move for a second and tried to run two parallel systems in my head:

One, the impulsive desire to wave it or crush it.

The second is that you run the Advanced Common Sense!

The second system won! After defining the problem and assessing the situation, I understood that if there was no factor threatening the bee it would not be motivated to attack. So, I decided to freeze and not surprise it. A decision that made the bee fly away, leaving me calm and satisfied.

> **Advanced common sense works! Use it!**

232 | Dr. Tuvia Rinde, PhD.

A FEW MONTHS LATER....

A new morning! The sun is shining. I'm on my way to an important meeting in the provincial city, and I am optimistic about the prospect of having a new project again. After about half a mile of a quick walk, and just a minute before the scheduled time, I arrive at the building. While moving toward the elevators, I look at all the doors to make sure there is no sign of work\maintenance issues and no light is off. Before pressing the elevator button to the 6th floor, I record the number and location of the elevator I entered. I press the floor button, the door closes, and again I am stuck in the elevator on the entrance floor with the internal control panel disabled and inactive buttons.

Pressing the alarm button causes the security officer to ask me " in what elevator are you? It's not listed, and there are many elevators in the building!"

I swear, I've already been through this, even in the same building! This time I confidently answer, "I am in elevator # 5, the middle elevator of the three on the right when you look from your control desk!"

"Don't worry, I'll get you out of the elevator in a few

minutes" he says in a matter-of-fact tone and after a brief pause, he asks, "Say, have you worked in the control team of this building?"

And I answered with a smile, "No, but after the last time I got stuck in an elevator here for an hour and a half, I learned from my mistakes and used my common sense. I was more careful this time. Don't you remember the ridiculous scene when you were so surprised I was laughing after being rescued?

After thirty seconds, he opened the door with the master key and asked me with a shy smile, **"Say, where can I get a copy of your book "Common Sense for the Advanced? I haven't gotten stuck in an elevator, but I have a lot of other interesting things going on in my life."**

I pulled out a copy from my bag and gave it to him. He smiled again and said, "Listen, next time you come, tell me it is you and I will watch over you and follow the elevator until you reach the floor you need!"

Advanced common sense works! Use it!

Best wishes for successful implementation. I am sure you now have a toolkit that will benefit you your whole life.

Dr. Tuvia Rinde

EPILOGUE

For years, I have been in the field of various corporate and enterprise organizations.

The common sense method has successfully passed the sarcasm and ego cynicism tests of all sorts of experts and analysts—for a simple reason. It just works!

The method is effective in daily life as well as in professional and managerial aspects.

Life gave me the gift of being in a variety of industries, a gift that made me a" tailor" and not a "confectionary." A gift that created the ability to adapt the method of Advanced Common Sense for different corporate cultures, technologies and management tools.

Now you can do it too!

If you have trouble, you can invite me to lead you in embedding the common sense method as the most critical and useful tool.

I would love to do so.
With dedication and care,

Dr. Tuvia Rinde

tuvia.rinde@gmail.com. www.drtuviarinde.com.
972532234805

Made in the USA
Monee, IL
20 December 2020